GREAT SEX

GUIDE

Guide for Beginners to Boost Your Sexual Energy, Make Incredible Sex, Learn Sex Positions, Have a Great Sex Life.

Explore Your Fantasies with Spectacular Experiences. Sexuality Guide.

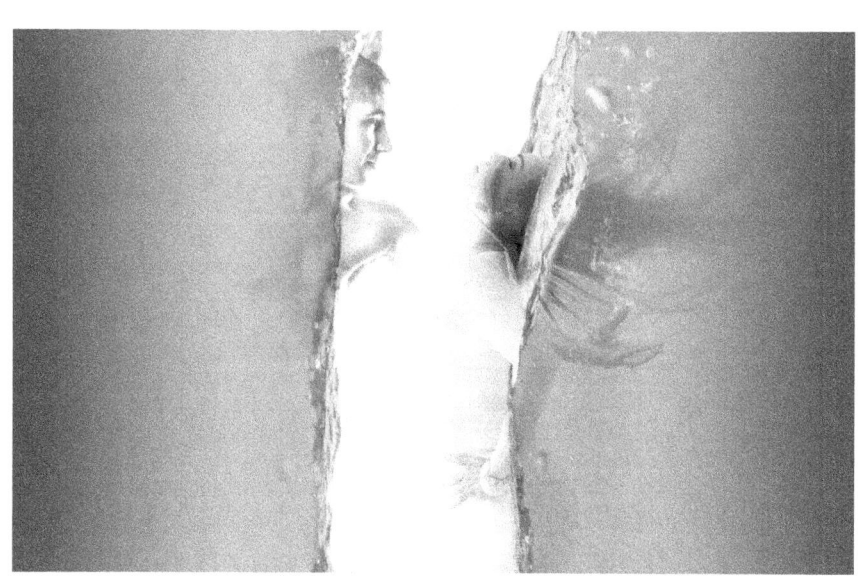

Table of Contents

Introduction 7

Chapter 1: Great Sex Unzipped 9

Chapter 2: Understanding Female Orgasm 16

Chapter 3: Unleashing Your "Everyday Sensuality" 22

Chapter 4: How Exercise and Food Can Improve Your Sex Life 28

Chapter 5: Simple Strategies for Stronger Erections 37

Chapter 6: Techniques to Delay Ejaculation 44

Chapter 7: Man & Sexual Performance Anxiety 50

Chapter 8: 7 Things Men Should Know About Vaginas 56

Chapter 9: 7 Day Sex Challenge And Reignite The Spark In Your Relationship 63

Chapter 10: Causes and Treatment of Low Libido in Men 69

Chapter 11: Drop-Dead Great Sex - Easy As 1, 2, 3 75

Chapter 12: Tips to Improve Your Sex Life 81

Chapter 13: The Basics of Female Body Language 92

Chapter 14: Ways to Be More Adventurous in Bed 97

Chapter 15: How to Choose the Best Lube for Sex: Types of Lubricants, Pros and Cons 102

Chapter 16: 10 Ways to Use Lube During Sex 110

Chapter 17: How to use a vibrator and sex toys the right way115

Chapter 18: Captive Bead Ring - Body Piercing Jewelry....... 120

Chapter 19: Myths and Facts About Sex Toys 124

Chapter 20: Choosing a Sex Toy - Selecting the Right Material
....131

Chapter 21: Woman's Guide to Safe Sex Basics.................... 137

Chapter 22: How to Stay Sexually Connected During Infertility
Treatment... 153

Conclusion 161

The following Book is reproduced below with the goal of providing information that is as accurate and reliable as possible. Regardless, purchasing this Book can be seen as consent to the fact that both the publisher and the author of this book are in no way experts on the topics discussed within and that any recommendations or suggestions that are made herein are for entertainment purposes only. Professionals should be consulted as needed prior to undertaking any of the action endorsed herein.

This declaration is deemed fair and valid by both the American Bar Association and the Committee of Publishers Association and is legally binding throughout the United States.

Furthermore, the transmission, duplication, or reproduction of any of the following work including specific information will be considered an illegal act irrespective of if it is done electronically or in print. This extends to creating a secondary or tertiary copy of the work or a recorded copy and is only allowed with the express written consent from the Publisher. All additional right reserved.

The information in the following pages is broadly considered a truthful and accurate account of facts and as such, any inattention, use, or misuse of the information in question by the reader will render any resulting actions solely under their purview. There are no scenarios in which the publisher or the original author of this work can be in any fashion deemed liable for any hardship or damages that may befall them after undertaking information described herein.

Additionally, the information in the following pages is intended only for informational purposes and should thus be thought of as universal. As befitting its nature, it is presented without assurance regarding its prolonged validity or interim quality. Trademarks that are mentioned are done without written consent and can in no way be considered an endorsement from the trademark holder.

Introduction

When you look for information, you should keep an open mind and accept your limitations. If the information you seek does not fit in with your way of thinking or acceptance levels, you may shrug your way out and look for material that does not involve much participation from your end. Every sexual encounter need not be the same. You can try out variations, plan themes and generally make the experience special.

If you arm yourself with a good sex guide, you can expect the unexpected. You learn the art of making proper conversation to set the pace for the evening. You can get your partner in the mood, by telling her how hot you are getting, or by just mentioning that sexy negligee she wore when you were with her last. Subconsciously, she is planning her moves to make you feel hornier. It is up to you to create the right ambiance and mood for the evening.

If you have zoned in the right guide, you will know what moves to make when she arrives, what foods to dish out to remove those inhibitions, which areas to tease and which to fondle and stroke. Be the complete master by following instructions from a good sex guide and making the evening memorable for both of you. Be consistent and gentle and try not to prolong the duration of your love making by not prematurely ejaculating.

Some guides tell you that if you ejaculate quickly, then you have time to work on her leisurely before you are sufficiently aroused. This may help to allow her to reach her orgasmic peaks and provoke her to join in the extended love game with abandon.

Chapter 1: Great Sex Unzipped

People always ask, what is great sex? What does great sex for men and women look like? We have studied numerous sex survey results and there are some consistent themes...

Great Sex

People always ask, what is great sex? What does great sex for men and women look like? We have studied the numerous sex survey results including those from AskMen, Cosmopolitan, ABC News, and iVillage over the past decade and, although there are some differences in men's and women's sexual desires (see below), there are some consistent themes when people talk about great sex for men and women:

- ➢ An emotional bond between partners reduces anxiety, increases the desire to provide their partner pleasure and improves overall sexual gratification.
- ➢ Communication is important for learning about one another's sexual desires and turn-offs.
- ➢ Experimentation keeps sex exciting. New positions, role playing, toys, and beyond helps couples enhance their sex lives.

> Great sex for men and women is usually accompanied by great orgasms for both partners.

The one factor of great sex discussion where the surveys reveal definitive information is with orgasms.

Orgasms - A Key to Great Sex

Comparing survey data from ABC News about sexual enjoyment and orgasms, men and women who says that they "always have orgasms" also answer that they "enjoy sex a great deal" 87% of the time while those that say that they "have orgasm less often" answer that they "enjoy sex a great deal" only 46% of the time. Although controversial, reaching orgasm during sex is a key component to sexual pleasure for both men and women but this orgasm gap is often a source of sexual dissatisfaction among couples. Of the most commonly discussed factors for an "exciting" sex life, the only one that was physical in nature was "frequency of orgasms".

How Men Define Great Sex

Men generally need three conditions for great sex. The first is his partner's sexual energy towards him. A man thrives on his partner showing a great passion to be satisfied sexually. Nothing turns on a man more than a partner whose sexual appetite for him is really strong.

The second is pleasing his partner. A man feels great satisfaction knowing that he is providing sexual gratification to his partner. The opposite is also true. Men also suffer from "performance anxiety" and embarrassment by not satisfying his partner.

The third is an intense orgasm that releases his sexual energy. As a general rule, the more time a man spends with various forms of sexual stimulation prior to orgasm, the more intense that orgasm will be. For a man, great sex includes a passionate partner who he completely satisfies and ends in an explosive orgasm.

How Women Define Great Sex

Most women also include an orgasm (or two or three) in their definitions of great sex but it's more about the entire experience. It starts with romance while the clothes are still on and continues on past male orgasm - substitute sleeping with cuddling!

A common complaint from women about men is that they're in a hurry to get to the end result. Women need time to warm up both physically and emotionally in order to really enjoy sex. It's not uncommon for many women to take 40 minutes to reach orgasm and they can feel self-conscious about it and not enjoy the process, even faking an orgasm so her partner will feel gratified. In an iVillage survey of what women want from their men in bed, 22% want more oral sex, 32% want "hear more loving things", 35% said more foreplay and 28% said that they wanted their men to last longer. Great sex for women starts slowly, proceeds slowly, and continues after orgasm.

Being a great lover means becoming a great lover to your particular partner, and that requires doing something very difficult: opening your mouth."

Great Sex Tip 1: Take Up Pillow Talk

Right. The mouth. Useful for kissing and other orally administered forms of arousal (none of which should be underestimated), it's also a tool for communication. Try it. Tell her what you want. Ask her what she likes. Shoot for trust and openness.

"If you get to know yourself and your partner, you'll have a much more erotic and explosive sexual relationship," says Joy Davidson, a New York-based psychologist and sexologist, and the author of Fearless Sex.

Great Sex Tip 2: Don't Believe Locker Room Talk

When men do talk, they often puff themselves up to their peers. Less apt than women to discuss their insecurities and more inclined to exaggerate their exploits, men paint distorted pictures of their sex lives for one another.

"A lot of men wind up thinking that their sex life is missing something, that other men are having wilder sex or more frequent sex," Davidson says. "They have a sense that the pleasure ship has sailed and left them behind."

According to Michael Castleman, a San Francisco-based sex expert and author of Great Sex: A Man's Guide to the Secret Principles of Total-Body Sex, the average frequency of sex in committed long-term relationships is roughly once every 10 days.

Great Sex Tip 3: Don't Compare Your Sex Life With Porn

Not everything men know about sex they learned from pornography. But a lot of it they did. And that can be a problem. Populated as it is by flawlessly formed women and men with etched abs and equine endowments, adult entertainment makes many guys wonder: What am I doing wrong? Or, more to the point: What's wrong with me?

"One of the most destructive myths of porn is that it convinces so many guys that they're too small," Castleman says. "They forget that pornography is self-selecting...These are not average men. They're the extreme end of the scale."

Some of the other fictions that porn perpetuates are the idea that women are always primed and ready ("in the real world," Davidson says, "people do say 'no'"); that the same moves work on every partner; that satisfying sex always culminates in orgasm.

13

Great Sex Tip 4: Focus on Pleasurable Sensations

While we're on driving, let's talk about commutes. And cubicles. And computers. And the demands and distractions of our daily lives.

Stress is an enemy of great sex. So is anxiety about performance. Minimizing both helps maximize your enjoyment of your partner. "If we can quiet our monkey-minds, put a stop to that ceaseless inner-chatter, we can open ourselves up to better sex," Britton says.

Great Sex Tip 5: Focus Less on Size and More on Other Matters

There are plenty of women for whom it absolutely does. But I prefer to focus on the idea of the right fit."

No two people are built the same, and it helps to have compatible body parts. For some women, men of modest size may be a perfect fit. It's a matter of physiology and personal preference. But perfect-fitting penetration isn't the only path to satisfying sex. Focus on foreplay. Concentrate on kissing, cooing, caressing -- the full panoply of sexual pleasure giving.

"A lot of women are very responsive to a man's voice during lovemaking," Davidson says. "If a man has verbal facility and can entice a woman through his voice, that can become a powerful part of his repertoire.

Chapter 2: Understanding Female Orgasm

Sex is one of the basic pleasures of life, but the orgasm is anything but simple — especially for people with vaginas.

The complexity begins with your anatomy. While you probably know that generally, your journey to orgasm starts with vaginal or clitoral stimulation, you might not realize that there's still debate among researchers about the exact anatomy of the clitoris. The most visible part of this intriguing organ is the small bundle of extra-sensitive nerve endings that sits right underneath where the two inner labia meet up top. From there, the clitoris actually extends internally in two shafts that sit along either side of the vagina. Experts may still be mapping the clitoris in full, but pretty much everyone understands the sexual purpose: pleasure.

To understand your orgasm, you should also know that the vaginal canal is lined with the soft tissue of the mucous membrane covering layers of stretchy muscle. (This canal leads to the cervix, a narrow passageway that sits in front of the uterus. This is the long journey upon which sperm must embark in order to fertilize an egg. Some research suggests that the female orgasm may help improve your chances of getting pregnant by improving "sperm retention," but you have to time it right.)

During arousal, you'll notice your heart rate increase, your skin may begin to feel (and look) flushed, and your genitals will swell with blood. But you're also building up a lot of muscle tension throughout your body.

Once you reach orgasm, the muscles in your vagina, anus, and uterus involuntarily rhythmically contract and then relax. Hence that awesome feeling of "release."

At the same time, your brain is working up quite a potent cocktail of chemicals. That includes the neurotransmitter dopamine, which is commonly associated with pretty much anything that feels good. But during an orgasm, you're also getting a huge release of oxytocin, which can promote feelings of closeness and empathy (among many other things).

The female orgasm is like a snowflake. No two are the same. Some females achieve orgasmic delight through genital stimulation, while others orgasm by having their hair washed at the salon. There are even known cases of females who experience orgasm when they brush their teeth or when their eyebrows are massaged.

But not every female is quite so lucky. In fact, nearly 20 percent of females are considered pre-orgasmic, i.e., they have never experienced an orgasm. But that does not mean they cannot experience orgasm. For this group, the path to orgasm may require a bit more patience, effort and alone time.

Here are six reasons why your orgasm may remain elusive and some suggestions for positive change:

Too performance focused

If you are focused too much on what you are doing and how well you are doing it, and not on how you are feeling then, chances are, your mind is getting in the way of experiencing sexual satisfaction. If you are immersed in analysing your "performance" or how your partner may be viewing you, then the focus is not sensation based – which can create a barrier to achieving orgasm.

Unsure of what you like

If you struggle to find words to describe your sexual likes and dislikes, you may not actually know what feels good for you. If the question "Tell me what you would like me to do to you" causes panic instead of delight, you might be in this group. But fear not! The solution is focusing on solo fun. Spend some time learning about your body and pleasuring yourself. Discovering where you like to be touched and how you like to be touched is a crucial first step in obtaining an orgasm. If you never masturbate, or you have only dabbled, then you may not have been able to unearth your body's secrets. It is also important to remember that only a small fraction of females experience an orgasm through penetration alone. Therefore, focusing all your attention on achieving an orgasm during intercourse or vaginal stimulation can have discouraging results for some.

Trouble communicating what feels good

If you are not being touched in a way that brings you pleasure, then reaching orgasmic delight with a partner is going to be difficult. If your partner(s) are not quite sure where your clitoris is, or how to touch it in a way that brings you pleasure, then learning how to communicate this effectively is important. Having good communication both in and out the bedroom is crucial for fostering good intimacy and pleasure-filled orgasms. If you are struggling to communicate, seeking the help and guidance of a counsellor or Sex Therapist may be a good first step.

Thinking too much

If your mind is wandering and you find yourself thinking about your body, work, or what you have to do after sex, then you are not staying present in the moment. Internal dialogue – that does not feed a fantasy or directly pertain to what you are doing or how you are feeling – is a distraction and can get in the way of an orgasm. Try to focus on how your body feels instead of what is running through your mind.

Past trauma or relationship concerns

Physical, psychological and emotional trauma can greatly affect your sex life. Seeking help from a counsellor or therapist in order to process through the trauma may be a crucial part of your path to orgasms. How happy you are in your relationship can also play an important role in your sexual satisfaction. If there is anger or resentment towards your partner, or don't feel safe (emotionally or physically) in the relationship, chances are you may find it hard to have an orgasm.

Stress, depression and anxiety

Overwhelming feelings of stress, depression or anxiety can also hamper your ability to be present during sex. If you are struggling to stay afloat from day to day then spending the mental and emotional energy needed to reach climax may be quite difficult. Reaching out to a counsellor or therapist may be a helpful first step in relieving these negative emotions and creating the kind of psychological wellbeing needed to relax and be present in your skin.

Underlying medical issue

Urinary tract infections, overactive bladder, yeast infections, clitoral adhesions, obesity, fatigue, constipation, STI's (formerly known as STD's), menopause, painful intercourse, birth control and other medications (such as antidepressants) are just a handful of things that can have a detrimental effect on a woman's ability to experience orgasm. If you feel as though the first few issues mentioned are not a problem for you, then perhaps there is a medical reason for why you are having difficulty reaching orgasm. The best thing to do in this situation is to contact your doctor and discuss your options.

Chapter 3: Unleashing Your "Everyday Sensuality"

Sensuality is the foundation for enduring human sexuality, a combination of the senses - touch, smell, sight, taste and sound...as well as internal energies and inner knowledge - that awaken in a person to fan the flames of passion for life and lovemaking. What does it really mean "everyday sensuality?" When one - man or woman - has unresolved tensions, arguments or hurt, it's difficult to be in touch with your spiritual and physical self. Stop for just a moment and close your eyes - can you feel your fingertips?

Are you aware of your body, the press of fabric against skin, any ache or pain, perhaps the brush of hair against the nape of your neck? Is your inner self experiencing feelings of awareness and gratitude? Are you going on frenetic energy today, a combination of to do list and caffeine? Everyday sensuality is easily defined as being aware of yourself and the world around you, in a powerful and self appreciative manner. Let's explore this idea, and how it relates to your inner sex goddess.

If you want to give a woman the night of her life and turn her into a blissed-out puddle of mush (that will be talking to her friends about you for weeks afterward), then look no further than the sensual massage.

Everybody likes sex, but the dynamic of a sensual massage is something entirely different. It's all about her receiving from you.

Whether it's for an anniversary, a date, or just a Tuesday night, there is nothing else that will leave her feeling so honoured, nurtured, loved, and turned on.

Even if you've never given a sensual massage in your life, if you follow these tips you are guaranteed to leave her with an unforgettable experience.

How To Give Her An Incredible Sensual Massage

1. Set the scene

Most women tend to be sensitive to ambience and context. In order for her to be able to completely relax internally, the outer environment has to be conducive to her relaxation.

> ➢ Make sure the room is well cleaned and tidy (laundry folded and put away, clean surfaces, etc.)
> ➢ Use only candle light
> ➢ Light some gentle/mild incense
> ➢ Layout soft blankets and pillows

> ➢ Play soft, ambient music
> ➢ Remove all distractions and make sure to turn off any beeping electronics

2. Prepare some oil

Use a natural, clean oil, since you're likely going to be using this on the outside AND the inside of her. Coconut oil is my personal favourite. Put a few tablespoons in a dish on the bedside table. Bonus points if you add a few drops of essential oil to create your own custom infusion.

Obviously, make sure the oil is comfortably warm to the touch before putting it on her skin so it doesn't startle her. If the oil is room temperature or less, rub your hands together vigorously for 5-10 seconds before putting them on her skin. You want everything to be comfortable and soothing. The last thing you want is her to dread your touch and wince, or get cold.

3. Use light, smooth touch

The key word here is "sensual". Sensuality is about provoking, stimulating, and teasing the senses. You're not there to perform targeted deep tissue to resolve chronic knee pain or treat her scoliosis. Your goal is to bring every ounce of her attention to her body and where your hands contact it.

Be progressive with pressure and intensity. The more light and drawn out the movements, the more arousing the sensual massage will be. If you need to get a sense of the rhythm, pretend you're massaging her in slow-motion, or like she's asleep and you're trying not to wake her up. Side note, if she does fall asleep at any point during the massage, that's fine. Don't take it personally or be offended. It just means that she's that relaxed, which is great.

Start with long, smooth full-palm strokes up her back and down her arms. Use the swirl technique to keep her nerve endings guessing (swirling your hands around lightly in an unpredictable, non-linear way over the whole body).

You'll develop better palpation skills with practice (palpation = detecting tension and problem areas with your fingers). When you find a tight place, spend some time making repetitive, deeper movements over it. Choose one spot and then slowly sink into it with a few firm fingers or a gentle elbow. Be very careful with this technique. It can be insanely satisfying and tension-busting, but also intense and painful. Go very, very slow, and listen to her breathing for cues as to how she's feeling moment to moment.

4. Communicate

Check in once in a while if the pressure is okay. Some parts will be more/less sensitive than others, so she may want your touch to change accordingly. Ask her if there are any areas that are calling out to her and yearning for more attention.

This will not only exponentially boost her satisfaction, but also help you learn what works and leave you feeling more confident overall that she's having a good time.

5. Escalate

Keep in mind that the arc of the sensual massage is a giant tease from initial feather-light touch on the back to full manual stimulation of her lady parts. Don't race. You want to build tension and anticipation. As you progress, gloss over her breasts and past her thighs but don't stop and spend ample time on her more obvious erogenous zones just yet.

Start with the head, neck, arms, hands, legs, butt, and feet. Then have her flip over and go further with her stomach, breasts, inner thighs, and finally genitals.

When you get to the vagina, work from the outside in, layer by layer. Take your time like you've never taken your time before. Lightly stroke the creases at the thighs on either side (if you didn't know, the clitoris isn't just a little bulb at the top of the vaginal opening, but is shaped more like a wishbone and runs down both sides of it). Stroke and gently tug at each labial lip. Caress everything. Take your time.

When you move to the inside, use the same philosophy of light, smooth touch and particularly focus on the G-spot, along the first few inches of the upper vaginal wall. Watch her breath and calibrate as you gradually build speed and intensity. As long as you're both having fun, rinse and repeat!

It's up to you where to go from there. Sometimes it can be a nice touch to keep sex entirely off the table. Making the whole experience just about her keeps this container of honouring and service more fully in tact, which will tend to make her feel extra special.

Just remember to take your time and tease. If it helps, keep a clock or your phone within view and draw the whole process out over an hour, at least.

Tip

Make sure you have your partner's consent before including anything overtly sexual in your massage. Check that she is comfortable with the level of intimacy throughout the massage and stop immediately if she asks you to.

Sharing a candlelit bath together before the massage will relax you both and get you in the mood for intimacy.

Chapter 4: How Exercise and Food Can Improve Your Sex Life

Every person wants to be fit, and every person also wants to have an awesome sex life. Fitness and sex life are two of the most important factors that determine the quality of life of a person. Unfortunately, most of the people all over the world are not fit.

The people are not fit because of the poor diet plan and lack of exercises. And, there are many people in the world who are struggling to have a satisfying sex life. And, a poor sex life is also the reason why there are many products like the male fertility booster in the market that promise to enhance the sexual performance of the people.

When it comes to the fitness, there are two things that first pop up in our mind, and i.e. foods and regular exercises. Unfortunately, the survey reveals that the majority of Americans lack basic nutrition information. And, the statistic shows that more than 2 out of 3 Americans are either overweight or obese, and the most common cause of obesity is an unhealthy lifestyle.

Furthermore, the survey conducted among 3,000 couples showed that around 6 out of 10 couples were not satisfied with their sex life. All the studies and statistics mentioned show how serious issues, fitness and sex life really are in the life of ordinary people.

Thankfully, there are natural ways to increase stamina and sexual performance along with products and medications that can solve the sexual problems of the people. In the next part of this article, we will discuss the relationship between fitness and sex life.

Focus on your fitness to improve your sex life

You need to change your lifestyle in order to be fit. Changing your lifestyle means subscribing to a better plan and getting involved in regular workouts. After changing your lifestyle, you will gradually improve your fitness level, which will eventually start improving your sex life. Here is how fitness can improve your sex life.

1. You will stay away from bad habits: There are certain foods and habits that can ruin your sex life, and staying away from them is one of the ways to enhance your sex life. Some bad habits like smoking and alcohol can not only damage your liver and lungs, but they can also suppress your libido, decrease your sexual performance, and also increase your chances of sexual disorders. The study conducted among erectile dysfunction patients showed that the patients who stopped smoking had improvement in their condition.

2. Self Confidence: One of the most important factors that determine the quality of sex life is self-confidence. The people with a healthy lifestyle are more likely to have a stunning body in comparison to those with a poor lifestyle. A stunning body makes people feel sexier. When a person has a stunning body, he/she feels sexier, which increases their sex drive? It greatly helps in enhancing the sex life of a person. Furthermore, exercises like pelvic floor exercises are a natural treatment for premature ejaculation (one of the common male sexual disorders).

3. Successful aging: There are many negative impacts of aging, and aging also has many negative impacts on a sex life of a person. Both men and women go through various physical changes due to aging, which affects their sexual performance. The good news is that being fit helps in countering many sexual issues related to aging. According to the study, there is a positive relationship between a level of sexual activity and the level of fitness.

4. More endorphins in the body: The fit people are found to have a higher level of endorphins in the body. It is because the fit people are usually active people, and the active people have enhanced production of endorphins in the body.

Endorphin is the hormone that enhances our mood and makes us happy.

And, happy people have a better self-esteem an increased production of sex hormones, which eventually improves their overall sex life. Furthermore, the people with a great body structure are also usually happier than unfit people.

1. Improved stamina: It is very crucial to have an optimum level of stamina in your body to carry out day to day activities. Like all other physical activities, you need to have storage of stamina in your body to spend a long time in the bed with your partner. If you do not have an optimum level of stamina in your body, then you will not be able to spend a quality time in the bed with your partner, resulting in a miserable experience. A proper diet plan and regular workouts greatly boost the level of stamina in your body, which allows you to satisfy your partner in the bed. And, it will enhance your overall sex life.

2. Increased body flexibility: You need a great stamina, and you also need a great body flexibility to perform well in the bed with your partner. I'm pretty sure that you would want to try many different sex positions with your partner and to perform many different sex positions; you need both stamina and body flexibility. The people with a higher level of fitness usually have greater body flexibility, which allows them to try out many different sex positions with their partner that will result in a greater sexual satisfaction.

3. Improved hormonal profile: Being fit means not only you will have a lean body, but you will also have a better hormonal profile. Having a high percentage of body fats can increase your sex hormone binding globulins (SHBG) in the body. It has a negative impact on your testosterone, which is a hormone that plays a crucial role in determining your sex drive. And, a high percentage of body fat also has a negative impact on your blood circulation, which leads to a restriction of the blood flow in the sexual organs. On the other hand, a healthy body has a better production of testosterone, which ultimately increases your sex drive. However, you should not spend a lot of time in workouts, as overtraining can decrease your testosterone.

4. Reduced stress level: Exercise is one of the best ways to manage your stress. A higher level of stress not only impacts your mental health, but it also ruins your sex life. A poor lifestyle can increase your stress, which decreases your sex drive. The study shows that the people involved in regular workouts have a reduced level of cortisol, a stress causing hormone, in the body. A better mental health leads to a better sex life.

Foods for circulation and stamina

Keeping the circulatory system in good working order is essential for sexual health. Better circulation can lead to an improved sexual response in men and women. This is especially true for the erectile response. Cardiac health is also vital for stamina.

In other words, if it is good for the heart, it is good for a person's sex life.

The American Heart Association recommend a diet that includes:

- ➢ a wide range of fruits and vegetables
- ➢ whole grains and plenty of fiber
- ➢ healthful oils, such as olive oil and sunflower oil
- ➢ seafood, nuts, and legumes

Research suggests that following this heart-healthy diet can improve certain aspects of sexual health.

Researchers studying the Mediterranean Diet, which follows similar lines to the American Heart Association's, found that people with metabolic syndrome who followed the diet had fewer problems with erectile dysfunction, otherwise known as ED.

Also, many of the foods featured in a heart-healthy diet, such as avocados, asparagus, nuts, seafood, and fruit, have associations with better sex in both traditional medicine and scientific research.

Foods to boost libido

Foods that can help people improve their libido are commonly called aphrodisiacs, after Aphrodite, the ancient Greek goddess of love.

Oysters are among the most famous aphrodisiacs in history. Their effects may be due to their zinc content.

Zinc is a mineral the body needs every day for many vital functions, such as cell metabolism, stamina, and regulating levels of testosterone. Testosterone is the most important male sex hormone.

One older study found that zinc might be helpful for treating ED in people with chronic kidney disease.

Oysters have more zinc than any other food per serving. Some examples of other foods that are high in zinc are:

- ➢ crab
- ➢ lobster
- ➢ red meat
- ➢ fortified breakfast cereal
- ➢ pine nuts

Foods to help maintain an erection

When a person has difficulty getting and maintaining an erection, doctors refer to it as ED. According to the Urology

Care Foundation, ED affects up to 30 million men in the United States.

Understanding the physical, mental, and emotional factors that contribute to ED can help people choose a diet that promotes better sex.

Factors that contribute to ED include:

- problems with blood flowing into and staying in the penis
- damage to nerve centers in the penis
- side effects of medication, radiation, and other medical treatments
- depression, anxiety, and stress

Tackling the underlying cause is the best way to treat ED. But another thing people can do is eat more fruit.

In one study, researchers linked a higher fruit intake to a 14 percent reduction in the risk of ED. The flavonoid content of many fruits may be responsible for this improvement.

Foods rich in flavonoids include:

- berries
- citrus fruits
- grapes
- apples
- hot peppers

- ➢ cocoa products
- ➢ red wine
- ➢ tea (green, white, and black)

Takeaway

Many people look to their diet to increase their sexual desire, improve their ability to have sex, and increase the pleasure they get from sex.

While research indicates possible links between particular foods and better sex, those seeking the best food for sex should ensure they are eating a balanced, heart-healthy diet.

Chapter 5: Simple Strategies for Stronger Erections

The penis is the most temperamental part of a man's body. It tends to get too excited for its own good. It responds poorly to illicit substances. It can show up in a big way at inopportune times, while retreating from duty when you need it most. As far as sources of pleasure go, it can be pretty damn frustrating.

Most men know their penis is not likely to hit a grand slam every time it steps to the plate. According to a study published in the American Journal of Medicine, 85 percent of men between the ages of 20 and 39 say they "always" or "almost always" can get and maintain an erection, which means 15 percent of men in the prime of their life have a hard time getting hard at least occasionally. The same study found that of men between the ages of 40-59, only 20 percent said they could get a healthy enough erection for sex most of the time. In other words, solid wood is far from a foregone conclusion.

Though you may never be able to predict how your penis will behave with 100 percent accuracy, there are steps you can take to make sure that when it comes time to perform, your erections are as healthy and strong as they can be.

1) Try a cock ring.

Did you know that a cock ring can help you maintain an erection? This O-shaped toy fits around your penis and helps keep blood in the shaft, where you want it. A cock ring also helps prevent venous leakage, a form of erectile dysfunction where blood flows to your penis, but has trouble staying there. (Giddy, a new cock-ring-like gadget designed to treat ED, may also help guys with venous leakage maintain stronger erections.)

There are four types of cock rings, all of which can help in the erection department:

- Adjustable rings
- Stretchy rings
- Vibrating rings
- Solid rings

2) Hit the gym.

According to Ryan Berglund, M.D., a urologist at the Cleveland Clinic, bloodflow is the key to a healthy erection, and there's nothing that encourages bloodflow like aerobic exercise. Not only does it keep you in shape, it builds the body's nitric oxide, which helps maintain erections.

While running is great, stay off the bike if you can help it. "Endurance cyclists who spend a long time on their bike seats may have more trouble with ED," says Erin Michos, M.D., an associate professor of Medicine at the Johns Hopkins University School of Medicine.

Those tight shorts can't help, either.

3) Put the cigarettes away.

In a study conducted at the University of Kentucky, researchers found that when asked to rate their sex lives on a scale of 1 to 10, men who smoked averaged about 5, while nonsmokers rated theirs 9.

One reason is that smoking is a known cause of impotence, and there's some evidence that smoking affects erection strength—and size. In one study, researchers found that smokers' penises are smaller than those belonging to nonsmokers.

"In addition to damaging blood vessels, smoking may cause damage to penile tissue itself, making it less elastic and preventing it from stretching," says Irwin Goldstein, M.D., a urologist at the Boston University medical center.

We have yet to hear a better reason to quit.

4) But keep a pot of coffee on.

Though few things are worse for your erection than a cigarette habit, coffee can actually help you out below the belt. A study by the University of Texas Health Science Center at Houston found that men who consumed the caffeine equivalent of 2-3 cups of coffee per day were less likely to suffer from erectile dysfunction than those who preferred to wake up with caffeine-free beverages.

5) Get a vasectomy.

If you're finished producing offspring (or you're sure you don't want kids), consider investing in permanent renovations at the sperm factory.

"The risk of a contraceptive failure can be a big source of anxiety for some men, especially those who've had a birth-control disaster—or a scare—in the past," says Karen Donahey, Ph.D., director of the sex- and marital-therapy program at Northwestern University.

That anxiety can, in turn, lead to erection problems—and cause the same vicious circle that makes performance anxiety such a mood killer.

But if there's no sperm, the risk of pregnancy is beyond minuscule: A properly performed vasectomy has an effectiveness rate of 99.9 percent.

6) Stay faithful.

It's common for men who start having affairs to stop having erections. So common, in fact, that doctors who treat erectile dysfunction often ask their patients if they're getting any action on the side.

Unless your wife knows about, approves of, and participates in your new sex life—in which case, we'd like to meet her—you're bound to feel at least a little guilty about it when you're with her. Guilt can turn to anxiety, and that can kill an erection.

7) Lose your gut.

Besides taking up residency at a monastery, having diabetes is the quickest route to a lifetime of celibacy.

In fact, more than 50 percent of all men with diabetes are impotent. The disease hits the penis with a double whammy. It accelerates the process of arterial disease, and it slows the transmission of stimuli along nerves throughout your body. And, trust us, a numb penis is not a happy penis.

Staying trim is the best way to avoid diabetes. If it's too late for that, be vigilant in checking your blood sugar (talk to your doctor about the best methods).

Men who are sloppy about controlling their levels have 70 percent more erection problems than those who stay on top of it, according to a recent Italian study.

8) Take it easy when you're thrusting.

One vigorously misplaced thrust is all it takes to rupture the corposa cavernosa, the elongated "erectile chambers" that run the length of your penis.

Don't believe us? Try aiming your erect penis at the trunk of a tree—it's roughly the same density as your partner's pubic bone.

A complete rupture will require surgery within 24 hours to stanch internal bleeding and reduce the risk of permanent damage. A partial tear isn't as serious, but it may cause problems later on. As the linings of the corposa heal over with scar tissue, they lose their elasticity—leading to curvature, pain, and eventually impotence.

By some estimates, more than a third of impotent men have a history of "penile trauma."

To protect yourself, be careful when she's on top. That's the position most likely to cause damage.

9) Walk more.

In one recent study, researchers found that men who walk just 2 miles a day had half the rate of erection problems of more sedentary men, says Dr. Goldstein. (Twenty minutes of jogging or 30 minutes of weight training will work, too.)

Deposits that clog or stiffen penile arteries can also wilt erections. "Guys tend to think of their arteries as simple pipes that can become clogged, but there's a lot more going on than that," says Laurence Levine, M.D., a urologist at Chicago's Rush-Presbyterian Medical Center. "The linings of those blood vessels are very biologically active areas where chemicals are being made and released into the bloodstream."

The more you exercise, the healthier, cleaner, and more flexible those linings become.

10) Get plenty of sleep.

Your penis needs as much shut-eye as it can get. Every night while you sleep, you have between three and five hour-long erections. You probably noticed this phenomenon the last time you had to pee at 4 a.m.

Those erections are not there just to make life interesting for your bedmate. They work to recharge your penis—keeping it well nourished with oxygenated blood.

"Theoretically, the more nocturnal erections you have, the more flexible your erectile tissue will become. And that may help keep erections strong as the years wear on," explains Dr. Goldstein.

Chapter 6: Techniques to Delay Ejaculation

Premature ejaculation is the most common ejaculation-related health condition. Premature ejaculation is when a person ejaculates or 'comes' too quickly during sex. There are a few ways to try and improve premature ejaculation, including medical treatments, techniques, and lifestyle changes.

What is premature ejaculation?

Premature ejaculation is a condition where a person ejaculates (comes) too quickly during sex. Premature ejaculation can affect up to 30% of men, and is split into 2 different kinds, lifelong (primary) or acquired (secondary):

 - Lifelong/primary – where the problem has existed since the first time a person has had sex
 - Acquired/secondary – where premature ejaculation is intermittent or starts later in life

International guidelines on premature ejaculation define it as when a man ejaculates within one minute of entering their partner. But, the average ejaculation time is around 5 ½ minutes. So, if you ejaculate much faster than this, you could think about ways to improve it if it's a problem for you.

What counts as having premature ejaculation?

Ejaculation can be called 'premature' if it happens less than 2 minutes into having penetrative sex. But, the official times for what's classed as 'premature' ejaculation can change between different countries, cultures, and healthcare experts. Still, most experts agree that if sex lasts less than 2 minutes, and ejaculation occurs, then it can be called a premature ejaculation.

Whether or not you decide to look for medical treatment for premature ejaculation is a personal choice. If your ejaculation time is causing you or your partner distress, you could look into treatment or techniques to improve it.

How common is it?

Premature ejaculation is the most common ejaculation problem and can affect up to 30% of men at some point during their lifetime.

There are several 'risk factors' which make getting premature ejaculation more likely.Men who are most at risk of developing premature ejaculation might:

> ➢ be under a lot of stress
> ➢ have depression
> ➢ be overweight
> ➢ drink too much alcohol

> smoke

There are treatments available for premature ejaculation specifically. But, if it's caused by another underlying health condition, you may need other medical treatments as well.

What causes different types of premature ejaculation?

There are two types of premature ejaculation, primary and secondary.

Lifelong (primary) premature ejaculation

Primary premature ejaculation will happen the very first time a person has sex, and will happen every time afterwards. Psychological factors are often common causes of lifelong premature ejaculation. This is compared to men who have secondary premature ejaculation, where the causes can sometimes be physical.

Causes of primary premature ejaculation include:

> Psychological issues: some men who have experienced childhood trauma related to sex can cause them to become overly anxious about sex
> Culture: an individual's culture can cause lifelong premature ejaculation, particularly if sex is taught to be inappropriate or shameful
> Conditioning: some men become conditioned when ejaculating, which can cause lifelong premature ejaculation. For example, some men condition

themselves to ejaculate quickly during adolescence to avoid being caught, which leads to ejaculating too quickly with a partner

Acquired (secondary) premature ejaculation

Secondary premature ejaculation is often caused by stress, anxiety, and/or depression. Psychological factors like these are all strongly linked with sexual dysfunctions, including premature ejaculation. Research has shown that in men who ejaculate prematurely, there is a strong link with depression. Other factors include relationship issues, personal conflicts, and performance-related anxiety.

There are also physical causes of secondary premature ejaculation, including:

- ➢ Thyroid problems
- ➢ High blood pressure
- ➢ Prostate disease
- ➢ Binge drinking
- ➢ Conditions like multiple sclerosis or nerve damage

Relationship issues are also seen as a common cause of premature ejaculation. Relationship causes of premature ejaculation can be a 'vicious circle', particularly if the partner is not supportive. This can lead to an even higher level of anxiety and fear of failure. If relationship problems are a cause of premature ejaculation, it may be due to:

> Different sexual needs

> Anxiety around sexual satisfaction

> Lack of communication

> Fear of sex

How to delay ejaculation

There are several self-help techniques for delaying ejaculation, like:

> Masturbating up to two hours before having sex

> Using thick condoms to reduce the sensation in the penis

> Having sex with your partner on top, so they can pull away when you are near to ejaculating

> Taking a deep breath to shut down the ejaculatory reflex

The squeeze technique:

> You or your partner masturbates you and stops before you ejaculate

> They then squeeze the head of your penis for 10-20 seconds

> They let go of your penis for 30 seconds and then resume masturbation

> Repeat this process several times before ejaculation is allowed to happen

The stop-go technique:

- ➢ Similar to the squeeze technique
- ➢ Your partner doesn't squeeze your penis though
- ➢ When you have built your confidence about delaying ejaculation, you can have sex, stopping and starting as needed

These techniques require practice to get right, but should help to delay ejaculation in the long term.

Lifestyle changes: if your premature ejaculation is related to certain risk factors, you might be able to improve it by making some changes. This might include quitting smoking, drinking less alcohol, or losing weight.

Conclusion

Premature ejaculation is very common. It happens to every man at some point. But if it happens frequently, you should talk to your doctor. There are many techniques you can use that may help prevent premature ejaculation. You should also talk to your partner. Often, your partner may feel responsible or disconnected. Talking about it can help put both of you more at ease. Also, your partner can help with the strategies described above for controlling your ejaculation.

Chapter 7: Man & Sexual Performance Anxiety

A man has erection problems if he cannot get or keep an erection that is firm enough for him to have sex. Erection problems are also called erectile dysfunction or impotence.

Most men have erection problems every now and then. This is normal. These problems can occur at any age. But they are more common in older men, who often have other health problems. Treatment can help both older and younger men.

This unpleasant experience is usually recorded in the man's memory and the next time he attempts to have sexual contact, he has thoughts that take the form of threat and fear. These thoughts are usually the following: "Will I achieve erection?"; "Will I make a fool of myself again?"; "If I have no erection, then something bad is goint on with me!". There is no way for a man to arouse sexually when having such thoughts; on the contrary, these thoughts induce fear and anxiety as the time for sexual contact approaches or while the intercourse is taking place.

However, ALL men's body is made up in such a way that, when the brain sends a warning signal for a potential danger or threat, fear prevails and then the body gets prepared on a biological level to cope with the risk. This means that high amounts of adrenaline are produced, increasing heart rate and vascular contraction; as a result, blood cannot fully reach and perfuse the penis, something which is essentially required to achieve erection. In other words, when a man is anxious and feels fear during intercourse, it is almost impossible for him to reach erection, and even if he does it is still very hard to maintain it. And then, it is most likely that both he and his partner will go through moments of discomfort, uneasiness, dissappointment, even despair. In this way another negative experience is recorded in the brain.

And this is the onset of a domino process. When the next sexual contact comes, the same thoughts (mentioned above) will be repeated, but this time he will be even more obsessed with them; there will be more fear and anxiety and, therefore, the possibility for failure will be higher. As a consequence, a whole 'vicious circle' starts on, which very often results in avoiding sexual contact and any circumstances that could potentially lead to sexual intercourse. Some men realise that the problem is due to anxiety and they try to convince themselves that "they should not think about it". Others try to 'rationalize' the situation and convince themselves that "they are calm and have no stress". However, as long as they refuse to accept the problem and ask for help, they end up thinking about it even more and, thus, the vicious circle remains there and perpetuates.

From the above it becomes clear that not achieving or losing erection when there is fear or anxiety is an ABSOLUTELY NORMAL function of the male organism. A man's body is constructed in such a way that there is good sexual function only if he is calm and at ease. In many cases, the one and only cause of erectile dysfunction may be sexual performance anxiety (mentioned above), which maintains the problem for months or even years. Many men cannot easily accept that their problem is psychological. This reflects some common viewpoints according to which psychological problems are signs of weakness and every man should be able to overcome them on his own. It seems that even the most mature and consistent men have deeply rooted convictions supporting that a real man should always achieve erection on any circumstances and shouldalways satisfy his female partner's sexual needs. Such convictions are the most fertile ground for creating and maintaining the so-called 'sexual performance anxiety'!

When there is organic etiology

In other cases, there may be organic etiology for erectile dysfunction and performance anxiety may aggravate the problem. Many diseases are related to erectile dysfunction, such as depression, hypertension, heart and circulatory problems, diabetes mellitus, multiple sclerosis, prostatic diseases.

Also related to erectile problems are various theraupeutic treatments, such as antidepressants and anxiolytics, antihypertensives, some surgical interventions of the prostate, bladder and intestines, hormonal therapy or radiotherapy for prostate cancer.

Whatever the case, it is particularly important that the man visits an expert, so as to identify and treat the cause of the problem. In many cases, the information the specialist physician collects is sufficient to differentiate whether the problem is due to psychological or organic causes. In some cases, however, there is need for specific examinations of the urinary, endocrine, vascular and nervous system, as well as laboratory testing.

The partner's role

Given that sexual intercourse involves the female partner as well, we should not forget that she herself also encounters her partner's erectile problem and probably she may also be experiencing her own 'vicious cirle'. Women usually start having thoughts such as: "I am not attractive for him anymore"; "Maybe there is another woman in his life"; "We will not be able to have children"; "My sexual life is over'" etc. Such thoughts are stressful and may lead to situations where the woman's sexual desire is reduced, she in in tension during intercourse and does not offer sufficient sexual stimuli to her partner. In the same way as it was described in men, women may also start experiencing unpleasant feelings and avoid sexual contact or there may be tension in the couple after every unsuccesful attempt, having negative impact on their everyday life and ultimately in their relationship.

The Treatment

When performance anxiety is the cause of erectile dysfunction, then it is essential to receive consultation and psychosexual therapy by experts. The specialist has to evaluate many factors that could possibly increase anxiety. For example, living conditions, general stress, relationship problems, other psychological problems (e.g. anxiety disorder), previous sexual experiences etc. After taking the man's history, the expert physician will suggest a theraupetic scheme, which in most cases lasts over 3 months.

The psychological intervention gives significantly better results when the female partner also participates in the process and, thus, the intervention is implemented in the couple as a whole. In many cases, the psyco-sexual therapy can be combined with pharmacotherapy that facilitates erection, i.e. phosphodiesterase inhibitors (PDE inhibitors). During the first crucial period, these drugs help the man/the couple to reset and start again their sexual life, giving the necessary time for the therapy to work. Very often these drugs are administered on a daily basis, so that the couple is not burdened with the stress of scheduling sexual intercourses and spontaneity is enhanced.

Through the therapy, the couple has the potential to improve not only their sexual function, but also their sexual communication and the quality of their sexual relationship. And it happens very often that, once the therapy is completed, the couple starts enjoying their sexual life even more than they had used to before the problem occurred!

Chapter 8: 7 Things Men Should Know About Vaginas

Of all the great things in life, sex can be one of the most rewarding.

When done correctly, regular sex can improve your relationship and sense of wellbeing. Not to mention it feels pretty darn good. But if you're a man who has sex with women, there's one thing you'll need to master before you can achieve the highest levels of sexual pleasure. It's the...

When it comes to the female reproductive system, things can get complicated fast. Yes, the vagina -- a term often used when people really mean the vulva -- can be delicate and complex.

A man's understanding of the vagina can dramatically affect his love life. Basically, if you're well-versed in vag, chances are your partner will want to get randy more often, thus leading to a slew of health benefits for the both of you.

Studies show that men who have sex at least twice a week have better heart health and lower risk of cardiovascular disease. Good sex also releases endorphins, which can reduce stress and improve sleep for everyone.

But better sex and foreplay don't magically happen overnight. That's why we put together a list of 7 things men should know about the vagina, so they can master the fine art of good sex.

1. When you say "vagina," you probably mean "vulva."

Technically speaking, vagina refers to the muscular, elastic canal which leads to the cervix and uterus. This is the "hole" where the penis or fingers are (usually) inserted and through which babies pass during birth.

"Vulva" is the term that describes all of the external organs that make up female genitalia. Basically, it's everything you're looking at when you're down there. The vulva includes the vagina, the pubic mound, the labia majora (the outer folds of the vulva) and labia minora (the smaller, inner folds), the opening of the urethra (the pee hole) and the clitoris (more on this very important part later).

2. Women can get erect, too.

Just as a man's penis swells with blood when he's aroused, women -- or, rather, their clitoris -- can become erect, too.

When a woman is turned on, blood flows to her clitoris, the small, round nub just above where the two inner lips meet. This causes the clitoris to swell and become sensitive to the touch. Be careful, though: The head of the clitoris can become overly sensitive and may retract underneath the hood to avoid further stimulation.

3. The clitoris is a powerhouse for pleasure.

With an estimated 8,000 nerve endings, the clitoris serves one purpose and one purpose only: to make a woman feel good. In fact, it's the only human organ that exists solely for pleasure, according to Dr. Hilda Hutcherson, a gynecologist with Columbia University and author of Pleasure: A Woman's Guide To Getting The Sex You Want, Need and Deserve.

And there's more to that beacon of pleasure than the little nub that peeks out. The clitoris has a body and two legs that extend within the body and run alongside the pubic bone.

These parts can be "very sensitive," Hutcherson told The Huffington Post. "I usually tell women and their partners to move around and try different positions [during foreplay and intercourse] to stimulate all the clitoral tissue and not just the head."

4. Just because a woman's vagina isn't lubricated, that doesn't mean she's not aroused.

While women are capable of lubricating naturally, Hutcherson says there are circumstances that can make it more difficult. For example, women may have a harder time lubricating naturally after menstruation. Certain medications and antihistamines also make lubrication more difficult, as do changes in hormones, birth control and age.

"Vaginal lubrication is one of those things that are really misunderstood by men," Hutcherson said, adding that most men don't realize that a woman can be aroused without having any wetness.

Some women may even take longer to become aroused and lubricated if they've been in a relationship for a long time. "In the beginning of a relationship, you lubricate very well and really quickly [because of all] the chemicals and hormones that are rushing through your body," Hutcherson explained. "Over time, those chemicals start to decrease after you've been with the same person for a while."

In either case, Hutcherson suggests that men should be patient and spend more time on foreplay if a woman isn't lubricated enough. "Sometimes it just takes a lot longer for a woman to get aroused," Hutcherson said. "Men don't understand why that happens."

5. Most women don't reach an orgasm with vaginal intercourse.

"Men like to think that there's something in the vagina that they're going to strike and cause an orgasm," Hutcherson told HuffPost. "They think women will have these mind-blowing orgasms from their penises alone, and it just doesn't happen that way."

In fact, a 2009 study revealed that about 75 percent of all women never reach orgasm from intercourse alone (that is, without the help of sex toys, or oral or digital stimulation). According to Hutcherson, foreplay and external stimulation can be far more important than penetration when it comes to women achieving orgasm.

She suggests beginning with gentle strokes to the clitoris and the labia, which can be very sensitive, but is often neglected. And if you really want to get a woman going, Hutcherson says that oral sex is "the easiest way for most women to experience pleasure."

6. When it comes to a woman's sexual stimulation, different strokes for different folks definitely applies.

One of the biggest mistakes a man can make when trying to please a woman is assuming that all women are stimulated in the same way.

"Every woman is different and they're not all going to respond in the same way," Hutcherson told HuffPost. "Women can have different parts of their bodies that are more sensitive than others." For example, one person may orgasm from clitoral stimulation, while another can only reach climax through penetration. The trick is to switch up the positions, techniques and areas of stimulation to see what the woman responds best to.

"Men shouldn't try to force a woman into having an experience that they think the woman should be having," Hutcherson said. "There's fun in exploring what gives a particular partner pleasure, discovering together what turns each other on.

7. This is how you find the G-spot.

The G-spot is a very controversial subject in the world of gynecology, and while some experts believe they have its exact location mapped out, others doubt that it even exists. Hutcherson believes the elusive G-spot is an area of glands near the urethra-side of the vaginal wall.

"The G-spot is not a spot," Hutcherson told HuffPost. "It's an area in the vagina that gives a woman the most pleasure, but it varies from woman to woman."

To find this "spot," Hutcherson offers her clients the following directions:

- ➢ Lubricate the fingers of the dominant hand and insert them, palm facing upwards, into the vagina.
- ➢ Reach the fingers all the way back until you feel the cervix.

- ➢ Once you hit the cervix, pull the fingers out slightly and rub the top of the vaginal wall where it feels most stimulating.
- ➢ Rub the area by curling your fingers, "like you're saying come hither against that front wall," Hutcherson says.
- ➢ Begin with light pressure then gradually add more pressure.

The most important thing to remember when handling, observing or adoring a vagina is to understand its keeper: The woman.

"Every person is different and every individual will have pleasure from different things," Hutcherson said. "That's the fun of being human.Try different things, have an open mind and be adventurous to find out what really works for both parties."

Chapter 9: 7 Day Sex Challenge And Reignite The Spark In Your Relationship

When it comes to sex, it can be easy to fall into the same old patterns. After all, when you're female, it's not always that simple to work out exactly what it takes to get your rocks off, and once you have figured it out, why would you risk changing it?!

But, as with any skill, hobby or past-time, it's essential to try new things to keep it fresh, interesting and satisfying. So, whether you're in a long-term relationship and you're looking for a little more variety, or you're just starting out and looking for a little bit of fun, we've got just the thing for you:

Day 1: Monday Night Massage

It may sound slightly cheesy, but a slow, gentle massage is a simple and effective way to bring you and your man closer together. Touch is essential in creating a close bond between many different species and as we relax, the body will release endorphins that create a feeling of well-being and happiness.

Before you start, it's vital to create a relaxing atmosphere. Make sure that the room is warm and you've got somewhere flat for him to lie comfortably while you work. Switch on lamps or fairy lights instead of the harsh light overhead and if you're using massage oils*, make sure they're close at hand and that you've laid down some towels as well.

You really don't have to be a master masseuse for a massage to be enjoyable either. Once they're comfortable, try alternating between stroking your partner's bare skin with your fingertips, lightly running your nails across them, and pressing slightly more firmly on the fleshier parts of his body, such as shoulders, back, and calves. Avoid putting pressure on his joints, though, as this can cause injury.

Then, swap! Now it's his turn to show you what he can do with his hands.

*Quick word of warning here: if you're planning for your massage to be a prelude to sex later on, make sure that you use a two-in-one water-based massage gel that also doubles as a lubricant. Essential oils aren't safe to be used during actual intercourse, plus they can also cause the rubber used in condoms to perish and break. Not so relaxing.

Day 2: Location, Location, Location

We all love our beds. They're comfy, cosy, and often the site of a lot of good memories (and dreams), but don't they get a bit... samey?

So tonight, rather than simply falling on top of one another as you fall into bed, make a conscious decision to get down and dirty somewhere else instead. Got the place to yourselves? Try on the kitchen table, or in the shower. Shared house? Stay in the bedroom, but lean yourself against the wall and give standing-up-sex a go instead. Varying the place means varying the position, which in turn means varying the sensation and who knows? You might just discover something you never knew you liked.

Day 3: Lucky Dipping

If there's something that you've been dying to try with your man, but haven't found the right time to bring it up, then this is your chance.

On three separate pieces of paper, each of you writes down three things that you've always wanted to try in (or out) of the bedroom, before folding them over and jumbling all six pieces of paper up together. If you're having trouble thinking of three different things that you haven't already tried, or you're not yet comfortable sharing those particular fantasies, pick three things that you already know you enjoy doing.

One of you then picks a piece of paper at random and provided you're both willing to give it a go, that's your task for the evening! If you fancy keeping the fun going a little longer, then pick as many more pieces of paper as you want and carry on going. Alternatively, just put them to one side to bring out another night (but don't peek, or you'll ruin the surprise...)

Day 4: Love Is Blind

Those of you with a man with a sweet tooth are going to love this one. Using a scarf, a tie, or a blindfold if you have one, cover your partner's eyes. Then grab something sweet and spreadable (such as honey or Nutella), and apply small dabs to at least five points on your body.

Guess what? He's now got to try and find them using only his mouth, and lick them off...

We would, however, advise against putting anything sweet anywhere 'south of the border', as it were. Glycerine can upset your body's natural pH balance and cause irritation, so by all means, use the honey to lead him there, but don't cover yourself in it like it's moisturiser.

Day 5: Rise and Shine

It's not always easy to find the time or energy for intimacy in the evening after a day of work or studying, so switch it up and set your alarm half an hour earlier than you usually would to surprise your partner with a morning quickie instead!

If you're both pushed for time after one too many taps of the snooze button, try jumping into the shower together and getting all 'lathered up' instead. Just make sure you've got a firm footing first - we all know how slippery those showers can be.

Day 6: Everything But

We don't mean that kind of butt. Or maybe we do.

It's easy these days to skip through the foreplay like you're skipping through YouTube ads, but tonight's the only night we recommend you don't have sex. At least, not in the fourth-base kind of way.

Start early in the day with a series of steadily-escalating flirty text messages that describe exactly what you're dying to do to each other. Then, when the evening comes, draw out the anticipation even longer with every kind of foreplay imaginable that doesn't end in intercourse. Kissing, touching, hands, mouths, even toys if you've got them; use every trick in your repertoire to satisfy each other instead. Now, how long's it been since you did that?

Day 7: Position Play

We've all got a firm favourite when it comes to sex positions, but instead of striking the typical pose, try adding a little twist for extra sensations.

If you're a fan of being on top, try bringing your knees up while keeping your feet on the bed instead in a squatting posture. This gives you greater control over the speed, angle and motion of your movement, making it easier to find what works best for you.

If you prefer him on top, try bending one knee up towards your chest and having your partner hold onto your ankle, while he rests his other hand on the bed above your shoulder. This change of posture allows for deeper penetration and greater external contact, increasing your chances of a clitoral orgasm as he moves.

For those who prefer doggy style, try positioning yourself at a point where you can rest your hands against a wall or bedframe, and tilt your body upright so that you're somewhere between kneeling and on all fours. This angle increases the contact of your partner's penis with your G-spot, plus it frees his hands up from supporting you, allowing him to use them for other purposes.

Chapter 10: Causes and Treatment of Low Libido in Men

Low libido is a term used to describe a decrease in sex drive that can interfere with sexual activity. While low libido can cause tension in a relationship, fostering doubt and guilt in both partners, it can often be treated if the underlying cause is identified.

Low libido should not be confused with erectile dysfunction (ED), although the two conditions can co-exist. Communication and honesty are needed for a couple to cope while identifying the possible causes. Treatment can vary and may involve psychotherapy, hormone replacement, lifestyle changes, or the adjustment of drug therapies.

Low libido can sometimes be caused by a single factor but is more often related to multiple factors that each contribute in their own way. Among some of the more common causes are low testosterone, medications, depression, chronic illness, and stress.

Low Testosterone

Low testosterone (hypogonadism) commonly develops as a man ages, but can also affect younger men for any number of reasons. Testosterone is the male hormone essential to development, strength, and sex drive. If the total testosterone drops below 300 to 350 nanogram per deciliter (ng/dL), the male libido can plummet, sometimes dramatically.

While testosterone replacement therapy may be useful in restoring the male sexual drive, it may increase the risk of blood clots and strokes in men with an underlying cardiovascular disorder. Sleep apnea, acne, and breast enlargement (gynecomastia) are other common side effects.

Medications

Medication side effects are common causes of low libido in men. These may include entire classes of drugs that can affect a man's sex drive to varying degrees. Common culprits include statins, beta-blockers, antidepressants, antipsychotics, benzodiazepines, and anticonvulsants.

Even over-the-counter drugs like Tagamet (cimetidine) can cause problems if taken for long periods of time. Stopping or changing the suspected drug may reverse the condition, although this is not always possible with certain chronic medications. A dose adjustment may also help. As always, do not change medication or dosage without first talking to your physician.

Depression

Depression and low libido may go hand-in-hand. Depression is often the cause of a reduced sex drive but may also be the consequence, making a tough situation worse. While psychotherapy may be effective in treating the depression, antidepressant medications can often exacerbate rather than improve the loss of libido. Switching drugs or reducing the dosage can sometimes help, but the side effects aren't immediate and skipping or delaying a dose won't help. If you are depressed, it is important to discuss your libido with your doctor and to talk about how medications may impact your sex drive.

Chronic Illness

Chronic illness can take a toll on your sex drive both physically and emotionally. This is especially true with conditions for which there is chronic pain or fatigue, including rheumatoid arthritis, fibromyalgia, cancer, and chronic fatigue syndrome.

When it comes to chronic illness and the loss of sexual function, there is rarely a straight line between cause and treatment. On the one hand, chronic illness is associated with an increased risk of depression, while on the other, it can directly interfere with hormonal, neurological, or vascular functions central to the male sex drive.

Moreover, the medications used to treat the chronic condition (such as chemotherapy or cardiovascular drugs) may directly impair the male libido. As such, your doctor may need to explore the cause both from the perspective of the chronic illness and irrespective of the chronic illness. In some cases, multiple doctors may be needed.

Stress and Sleep Disorders

While stress can impair sexual interest by literally driving you to distraction, its effect on the sex drive is more insidious. Stress triggers the production of cortisol, a hormone that functions rather like a body's built-in alarm system. Cortisol not only causes the constriction of blood vessels, contributing to ED, it can also cause a precipitous drop in testosterone.

Stress is also linked to insomnia and other sleep abnormalities, which can increase the risk of fatigue and leave you less interested in sex. There is even some evidence that elevated cortisol level may increase the risk of obstructive sleep apnea (OSA), a condition associated with the reduction of daytime testosterone by anywhere from 10 to 15 percent.

Treatment may involve stress management techniques and the use of positive airway pressure and improved sleep hygiene to treat conditions like OSA and insomnia. If the stress is associated with an anxiety disorder, medications may be needed, some of which (like benzodiazepines) may enhance rather than alleviate low libido.

Lifestyle

There are lifestyle factors that may contribute significantly to low libido in men. These tend to more readily remedied by simply changing or stopping the behavior. Among them:

Smoking not only directly increases the risk of ED but indirectly impairs sexual arousal, according to a 2012 study from the University of Texas Austin.

Alcohol, when used in excess or over the course of years, redirects enzymes needed to synthesize testosterone from the testes to the liver, resulting in reduced testosterone levels.

Obesity directly impairs metabolism and hormone function, resulting in significantly reduced total and free testosterone. By contrast, exercise and weight loss not only enhances mood and energy levels but also improves sexual function and self-image.

While the detrimental effects these behaviors are clear, it is never wise to "pin" low libido on single lifestyle factor without first conferring with a doctor to explore all other possible causes.

A Word From Very well

If the loss of libido is affecting your relationship, you need to take extra care to avoid directing blame at yourself or your partner. Instead, you would be well served to approach solutions as a couple, neither assigning it as his issue or my issue but rather one to which you both actively participate.

This requires open and honest communication about not only the physical symptoms of low libido but the emotional ones. Doing so allows you to identify which doctor or doctors are needed to diagnose, and hopefully, treat the condition.

This may include an endocrinologist, urologist, chronic disease specialist, psychiatrist, sex therapist, or other health professional. There may not be a quick fix, but, with time and patience, a solution may be found.

In the meantime, try to remind yourself that the loss of sexual desire is not the same thing as the connect emotionally and physically. By doing so, you can forge a closer bond and may even end up strengthening your relationship.

Chapter 11: Drop-Dead Great Sex - Easy As 1, 2, 3

Drop dead great sex is the sex that is so intense, and flat out going for the pure pleasure of it that both parties are left wiped out. This is a great feeling and while few do, anybody can experience great sex.

Some people have no problem talking about it while others avoid the topic altogether. Well today we will explore the topic of sex and how to have drop dead great sex!

What if there was a way you could enjoy great sex any day? Just imagine what it will feel like to live the dream, living with the relaxation and confidence of a lover a million times better than your hard up friends by the way, and all the while knowing the pleasure is finally attainable?

Imagine what it would be like and feel the feeling of having just what you want now.

The Simple Steps

➢ Know your partner - sex with a stranger is like working with a temp agencies.

➢ Avoid casual sex with strangers, there is nothing casual about sex with strangers.

➤ Learn the easy relationship strategies for success.

ONE

Know your partner - In order to have mind blowing sex, you must have a team player, one who likes the same sport. You must know the art of give and take in the relationship of sex. Some making up will need to be perfected. We all know the magic of making up!

TWO

Avoid casual sex much like the above mentioned sport or craft, casual sex is for amateurs. The best sexual matches practice it with those who enjoy the same things. Casual sex is like trying to play football with a baseball player and doing so in a bowling alley.

THREE

Know and understand relationship strategies. A good line of communication and understanding with your partner is a must in order to find the hot intense areas to explore and have fun.

SECRET

Women and men are not much different. Look at it like this, a man is merely a women turned inside out. When either sex acts as if they think they should (by the cookie cutter standards) the individualize aspect that makes for great sex is ignored. Having a partner you feel comfortable sharing your likes and dislikes with makes for the best of partners.

Secret Code Any time you tell your interested partner, "I feel the key to great sex is great communication and I would love to try both with you" you have just said the magic words that are the code to great sex. You must talk the talk or you are doomed to look a fool.

Bottom Line Stop break ups, divorce or lovers rejection by learning the magic of making up! Many of us have the perfect partner, we just need some repair work to get back to the magic. All relationships take work. It's what you don't know about making up that gets you broke up and lonely.

10 Huge Mistakes Men Make In Bed That Stop Them From Giving Their Women Great Sex

1. They Don't Realize They Are Lousy Lovers

This is the biggest mistake most men make in the bedroom.

They fail to realize (or at least won't do anything about) the fact that they are lousy or 'average' lovers. In other words -- they refuse to work on themselves.

This attitude guarantees that most men will never give their women great sex.

2. They Don't Understand A Woman's Potential For Wild Sexuality

Many men think that women are the less sexual of the two sexes, but nothing could be further from the truth.

This belief prevents most men from ever truly exploring their woman's sexual potential and therefore -- they never release it and never give their woman great sex.

3. They Fail To Realize That Women Only Want Great Sex

Women love sex, but they only want great sex.

Most men give average sex and that's a huge mistake because it causes their woman's sex-drive to decline and problems start arising in the relationship -- both inside the bedroom and outside of it.

4. They Do The Same Things Over and Over Again

Many men make the mistake of doing the same things over and over again in bed. In other words -- they allow the sex to become BORING.

Given the FACT that women only like fun, interesting, exciting and ultimately... great sex -- this is a HUGE MISTAKE.

5. They Don't Give Their Women Enough Foreplay

Many men try to avoid the starter and skip straight to the 'main course'. At a restaurant this may be a valid approach but in bed it's a disaster.

When men fail to give their women enough foreplay it reduces the pleasure that their women get from the whole sexual experience. And that's not good.

6. They Don't Talk Dirty

Women need to hear a man's voice during sex. Period.

But most men don't talk dirty and they therefore ruin their chances of ever giving their women great sex. Great sex needs DIRTY TALK.

7. They Don't Understand That Women Are Sexually Submissive

When men fail to realize that women are sexually submissive they don't realize that they need to be SEXUALLY DOMINANT.

Every woman wants her man to be sexually dominant and therefore, this is a huge mistake. Following on...

8. They Don't Take Control And Lead Their Women

To be sexually dominant a man needs to TAKE CONTROL and lead his woman in the bedroom. When he doesn't, it's a 'turn off' for his woman and she won't take him as seriously as she needs to in order to get 'totally lost' in the experience and have great sex.

9. They Don't Obey The Law That 'Women Are Creatures Of Sexual Reciprocation'

Women are creatures of sexual reciprocation, meaning that they give back as good as they get in the bedroom. Most men get frustrated because their women don't want to give blow jobs, have anal sex and do all the other dirty stuff that most men dream about.

But the truth is that women do want to do those things -- but only with the RIGHT MAN. A man who first blows her mind and gives her INCREDIBLE PLEASURE.

10. They Fail To Give Their Women Vaginal Orgasms

In order to truly satisfy a woman in the bedroom, a man should give his woman vaginal orgasms during intercourse. It is a mistake not to.

Given that 99% of men fail to do this, 99% of men are failing to give their women GREAT SEX. Once you realize this, it becomes much more obvious as to why many women are bored of the sex they have with their man and many CHEAT or 'play away' with another man.

Chapter 12: Tips to Improve Your Sex Life

Whether the problem is big or small, there are many things you can do to get your sex life back on track. Your sexual well-being goes hand in hand with your overall mental, physical, and emotional health. Communicating with your partner, maintaining a healthy lifestyle, availing yourself of some of the many excellent self-help materials on the market, and just having fun can help you weather tough times.

Enjoying a satisfying sex life

Sex. The word can evoke a kaleidoscope of emotions. From love, excitement, and tenderness to longing, anxiety, and disappointment—the reactions are as varied as sexual experiences themselves. What's more, many people will encounter all these emotions and many others in the course of a sex life spanning several decades.

But what is sex, really?

On one level, sex is just another hormone-driven bodily function designed to perpetuate the species. Of course, that narrow view underestimates the complexity of the human sexual response. In addition to the biochemical forces at work, your experiences and expectations help shape your sexuality.

Your understanding of yourself as a sexual being, your thoughts about what constitutes a satisfying sexual connection, and your relationship with your partner are key factors in your ability to develop and maintain a fulfilling sex life.

Talking to your partner

Many couples find it difficult to talk about sex even under the best of circumstances. When sexual problems occur, feelings of hurt, shame, guilt, and resentment can halt conversation altogether. Because good communication is a cornerstone of a healthy relationship, establishing a dialogue is the first step not only to a better sex life, but also to a closer emotional bond. Here are some tips for tackling this sensitive subject.

Find the right time to talk. There are two types of sexual conversations: the ones you have in the bedroom and the ones you have elsewhere. It's perfectly appropriate to tell your partner what feels good in the middle of lovemaking, but it's best to wait until you're in a more neutral setting to discuss larger issues, such as mismatched sexual desire or orgasm troubles.

Avoid criticizing. Couch suggestions in positive terms, such as, "I really love it when you touch my hair lightly that way," rather than focusing on the negatives. Approach a sexual issue as a problem to be solved together rather than an exercise in assigning blame.

Confide in your partner about changes in your body. If hot flashes are keeping you up at night or menopause has made your vagina dry, talk to your partner about these things. It's much better that he know what's really going on rather than interpret these physical changes as lack of interest. Likewise, if you're a man and you no longer get an erection just from the thought of sex, show your partner how to stimulate you rather than let her believe she isn't attractive enough to arouse you anymore.

Be honest. You may think you're protecting your partner's feelings by faking an orgasm, but in reality you're starting down a slippery slope. As challenging as it is to talk about any sexual problem, the difficulty level skyrockets once the issue is buried under years of lies, hurt, and resentment.

Don't equate love with sexual performance

Create an atmosphere of caring and tenderness; touch and kiss often. Don't blame yourself or your partner for your sexual difficulties. Focus instead on maintaining emotional and physical intimacy in your relationship. For older couples, another potentially sensitive subject that's worth discussing is what will happen after one partner dies. In couples who enjoy a healthy sex life, the surviving partner will likely want to seek out a new partner. Expressing your openness to that possibility while you are both still alive will likely relieve guilt and make the process less difficult for the surviving partner later.

Using self-help strategies

Treating sexual problems is easier now than ever before. Revolutionary medications and professional sex therapists are there if you need them. But you may be able to resolve minor sexual issues by making a few adjustments in your lovemaking style. Here are some things you can try at home.

Educate yourself. Plenty of good self-help materials are available for every type of sexual issue. Browse the Internet or your local bookstore, pick out a few resources that apply to you, and use them to help you and your partner become better informed about the problem. If talking directly is too difficult, you and your partner can underline passages that you particularly like and show them to each other.

Give yourself time. As you age, your sexual responses slow down. You and your partner can improve your chances of success by finding a quiet, comfortable, interruption-free setting for sex. Also, understand that the physical changes in your body mean that you'll need more time to get aroused and reach orgasm. When you think about it, spending more time having sex isn't a bad thing; working these physical necessities into your lovemaking routine can open up doors to a new kind of sexual experience.

Use lubrication. Often, the vaginal dryness that begins in perimenopause can be easily corrected with lubricating liquids and gels. Use these freely to avoid painful sex—a problem that can snowball into flagging libido and growing relationship tensions. When lubricants no longer work, discuss other options with your doctor.

Maintain physical affection. Even if you're tired, tense, or upset about the problem, engaging in kissing and cuddling is essential for maintaining an emotional and physical bond.

Practice touching. The sensate focus techniques that sex therapists use can help you re-establish physical intimacy without feeling pressured. Many self-help books and educational videos offer variations on these exercises. You may also want to ask your partner to touch you in a manner that he or she would like to be touched. This will give you a better sense of how much pressure, from gentle to firm, you should use.

Try different positions. Developing a repertoire of different sexual positions not only adds interest to lovemaking, but can also help overcome problems. For example, the increased stimulation to the G-spot that occurs when a man enters his partner from behind can help the woman reach orgasm.

The G-spot

The G-spot, or Grafenberg spot, named after the gynecologist who first identified it, is a mound of super-sensitive spongelike tissue located within the roof of the vagina, just inside the entrance. Proper stimulation of the G-spot can produce intense orgasms. Because of its difficult-to-reach location and the fact that it is most successfully stimulated manually, the G-spot is not routinely activated for most women during vaginal intercourse. While this has led some skeptics to doubt its existence, research has demonstrated that a different sort of tissue does exist in this location.

You must be sexually aroused to be able to locate your G-spot. To find it, try rubbing your finger in a beckoning motion along the roof of your vagina while you're in a squatting or sitting position, or have your partner massage the upper surface of your vagina until you notice a particularly sensitive area. Some women tend to be more sensitive and can find the spot easily, but for others it's difficult.

If you can't easily locate it, you shouldn't worry. During intercourse, many women feel that the G-spot can be most easily stimulated when the man enters from behind. For couples dealing with erection problems, play involving the G-spot can be a positive addition to lovemaking.

Oral stimulation of the clitoris combined with manual stimulation of the G-spot can give a woman a highly intense orgasm.

Write down your fantasies. This exercise can help you explore possible activities you think might be a turn-on for you or your partner. Try thinking of an experience or a movie that aroused you and then share your memory with your partner. This is especially helpful for people with low desire.

Do Kegel exercises. Both men and women can improve their sexual fitness by exercising their pelvic floor muscles. To do these exercises, tighten the muscle you would use if you were trying to stop urine in midstream. Hold the contraction for two or three seconds, then release. Repeat 10 times. Try to do five sets a day. These exercises can be done anywhere—while driving, sitting at your desk, or standing in a checkout line. At home, women may use vaginal weights to add muscle resistance. Talk to your doctor or a sex therapist about where to get these and how to use them.

Try to relax. Do something soothing together before having sex, such as playing a game or going out for a nice dinner. Or try relaxation techniques such as deep breathing exercises or yoga.

Use a vibrator. This device can help a woman learn about her own sexual response and allow her to show her partner what she likes.

Don't give up. If none of your efforts seem to work, don't give up hope. Your doctor can often determine the cause of your sexual problem and may be able to identify effective treatments. He or she can also put you in touch with a sex therapist who can help you explore issues that may be standing in the way of a fulfilling sex life.

Maintaining good health

Your sexual well-being goes hand in hand with your overall mental, physical, and emotional health. Therefore, the same healthy habits you rely on to keep your body in shape can also shape up your sex life.

Exercise, exercise, exercise

Physical activity is first and foremost among the healthy behaviors that can improve your sexual functioning. Because physical arousal depends greatly on good blood flow, aerobic exercise (which strengthens your heart and blood vessels) is crucial. And exercise offers a wealth of other health benefits, from staving off heart disease, osteoporosis, and some forms of cancer to improving your mood and helping you get a better night's sleep. Also, don't forget to include strength training.

Don't smoke. Smoking contributes to peripheral vascular disease, which affects blood flow to the penis, clitoris, and vaginal tissues. In addition, women who smoke tend to go through menopause two years earlier than their nonsmoking counterparts. If you need help quitting, try nicotine gum or patches or ask your doctor about the drugs bupropion (Zyban) or varenicline (Chantix).

Use alcohol in moderation. Some men with erectile dysfunction find that having one drink can help them relax, but heavy use of alcohol can make matters worse. Alcohol can inhibit sexual reflexes by dulling the central nervous system. Drinking large amounts over a long period can damage the liver, leading to an increase in estrogen production in men. In women, alcohol can trigger hot flashes and disrupt sleep, compounding problems already present in menopause.

Eat right. Overindulgence in fatty foods leads to high blood cholesterol and obesity—both major risk factors for cardiovascular disease. In addition, being overweight can promote lethargy and a poor body image. Increased libido is often an added benefit of losing those extra pounds.

Use it or lose it. When estrogen drops at menopause, the vaginal walls lose some of their elasticity. You can slow this process or even reverse it through sexual activity. If intercourse isn't an option, masturbation is just as effective, although for women, this is most effective if you use a vibrator or dildo (an object resembling a penis) to help stretch the vagina. For men, long periods without an erection can deprive the penis of a portion of the oxygen-rich blood it needs to maintain good sexual functioning. As a result, something akin to scar tissue develops in muscle cells, which interferes with the ability of the penis to expand when blood flow is increased.

Putting the fun back into sex

Even in the best relationship, sex can become ho-hum after a number of years. With a little bit of imagination, you can rekindle the spark.

Be adventurous. Maybe you've never had sex on the living room floor or in a secluded spot in the woods; now might be the time to try it. Or try exploring erotic books and films. Even just the feeling of naughtiness you get from renting an X-rated movie might make you feel frisky.

Be sensual. Create an environment for lovemaking that appeals to all five of your senses. Concentrate on the feel of silk against your skin, the beat of a jazz tune, the perfumed scent of flowers around the room, the soft focus of candlelight, and the taste of ripe, juicy fruit. Use this heightened sensual awareness when making love to your partner.

Be playful. Leave love notes in your partner's pocket for him or her to find later. Take a bubble bath together—the warm cozy feeling you have when you get out of the tub can be a great lead-in to sex. Tickle. Laugh.

Be creative. Expand your sexual repertoire and vary your scripts. For example, if you're used to making love on Saturday night, choose Sunday morning instead. Experiment with new positions and activities. Try sex toys and sexy lingerie if you never have before.

Be romantic

Read poetry to each other under a tree on a hillside. Surprise each other with flowers when it isn't a special occasion. Plan a day when all you do is lie in bed, talk, and be intimate. The most important tool you have at your disposal is your attitude about sexuality. Armed with good information and a positive outlook, you should be able to maintain a healthy sex life for many years to come.

Chapter 13: The Basics of Female Body Language

Learning to read female body language is a crucial skill. Understand female body language and you'll know when to take things to the next level with a woman – and when to slow things down. If you want to further develop this skill here are a few tips for reading female body language.

How to read body language

Reading female body language isn't really about spotting specific gestures and movements. It's about spotting changes in a woman's behaviors. So before you start looking for meaningful cues you've got to establish a "baseline" of her typical body language. How she deviates from the baseline will then give you a glimpse into how she is feeling.

For example, some women are naturally flirty and will do a lot of touching during conversation. So if you think a girl is interested in you just because she's touching you then you may be mistaken. What you want to look for is how a girl touches you compared with how she touches everyone else. If she touches you more frequently than everyone else, or in more personal areas (she touches your chest while just touching everyone else on the arm) that difference is how you know she's interested.

Signs of discomfort

One thing to keep in mind when looking for changes in female body language is if a woman "freezes up". This is a signal that shows discomfort, anxiety, or even insecurity. It's also one that can be spotted on any part of a woman's body. For example you may notice a woman playfully wiggling her feet under her chair – and then abruptly stop. Seeing this sudden change can let you know that something has made her uncomfortable.

Signs of freezing are a good thing to look for when you want to escalate with a woman. If a woman freezes up when you touch her (while avoiding eye contact) then it's a sign she's not yet ready to go any further. At times like this it's a good idea to step back and engage in some playful banter. Once she feels more comfortable with you, try again.

Signs she's engaged

The more positive body language you see from a woman the more interested and engaged she is. What is positive body language? If the girl is facing you directly and leaning in then she's showing you positive body language. If she's leaning away or angles her body away from you, she's showing negative body language.

The cool thing about positive and negative body language is that you can actually use it to create attraction with women. If a woman is giving you attitude or saying things you don't like you can respond simply with a bit of negative body language. Angle your body away and let her see that she's losing your attention. This shows you're a high-value guy who simply doesn't put up with that kind of behavior. As a result you're going to come across as that much more attractive to her and any other woman watching.

Barriers

Just like positive body language barriers can be a great way to see if a girl is gaining or losing interest in you. If she enjoys talking to you, feels comfortable with you, and is hoping to connect with you, then she'll start removing barriers. If she's feeling uncomfortable or distant, then she's going to construct barriers between you.

What do these barriers look like? They could be anything. A woman crossing her arms or holding a something across her chest (a drink, bag, book, etc) are all forms of barriers. If you're sitting across the table from a woman she may move her water glass directly between you to construct a barrier, or place it to the side to remove it. If she's sitting she can create a barrier by crossing her legs away from you, or open up to you by crossing her legs in your direction.

Signs she's flirting with you

The female body language signs most guys are interested in are the signs a woman is flirting with you. Things like strong eye contact, twirling her hair, and the positive body language signs mentioned earlier can all be signs the girl is flirting with you.

But as mentioned before merely spotting these behaviors doesn't mean the girl is definitely interested. What you want to see is an increase in these behaviors from her usual baseline. If you see multiple flirting signals that all deviate from typical behavior, then you can be far more certain that she's interested in you.

Microsexpression

Female body language can sometimes be tough to pick up on. Microexpressions are a perfect example. This is when an expression will flash across a woman's face for just a fraction of a second (men do it, too). If you're not paying attention they can be very difficult to spot. And that would be a shame as micro-expressions are a very accurate gauge for how a woman feels.

Any facial expression can briefly appear as a microexpression. If a woman is happy but trying to conceal it, it's only a matter of time until a smile briefly flashes across her face. If she's trying to hide a negative emotion that will eventually be revealed as well. She may briefly crinkle her nose (the sign for disgust) or curl just one corner of her lip back (contempt). If you see a microexpression that suggests one of these negative emotions it's probably time to change environments or topic of conversation.

FEMALE BODY LANGUAGE SUMMARY

As soon as you notice this type of behavior in a woman, you can surely tell that she's just giving you her sexual come-on because she's is erotically fascinated with you

Understanding female body language may take some time for some, yet if you follow your instincts, you will have no problem at all with this type of male/female communication strategy.

Chapter 14: Ways to Be More Adventurous in Bed

Do you sometimes ponder the question: "How do I get my wife to be more sexually adventurous?"

If yes, then you are at the right place because I am going to share with you exactly what has to be in place in order for your wife to be more sexually adventurous with you.

And, you should be excited because what has to be in place between you and your wife is well within your power to develop.

So speaking procedurally, below are some ways (i.e. requirements) to having a more sexually adventurous wife:

1. Turn The Heat Up

It's such a little thing, but most women are a lot more comfortable when they're not cold. If you want your husband to see you in lingerie, don't be shivering! Just put a space heater near your bed. That way you don't have to turn up the heat in the whole house.

2. Turn the Lights Low—or Use Candles

If you're nervous about him watching you, or about what you look like, then turn the lights low. You can still do a little "lingerie fashion show" without the lights blaring.

A little light is fun—men are visual, after all. But if you're nervous, setting softer light can go a long way to making you feel more at ease—and help you feel more adventurous.

3. Start with a Bath—or a Massage

Instead of just jumping in to sex, start with something that relaxes you and helps you feel intimate. After all, why are we scared to be adventurous in bed? Because it feels like all we care about is sex. Doing something that connects you more intimately first shows you that it's about the relationship. So cuddle in a warm bath. Take a hot shower. Have him give you a massage (while you're both naked!) Get relaxed and let yourself FEEL that he accepts you.

4. Create His Nights and Her Nights

Maybe there's something that he'd really like to try that you're not totally keen on. And you're worried that if you do it he'll want it all the time! Or you feel embarrassed to suggest that maybe you should try that tonight.

Here's the benefit: If you're feeling shy or embarrassed to try something new, psychologically you're "off the hook" because it's not YOU who is initiating this; it's him. And you know that you'll get your own preferences later. Then on the nights between the Saturdays you can just do what you would normally do.

Often we women actually want to do some of the things he'd want on "his" nights, but we don't want to feel like we'd have to be doing them all the time. Or else we're embarrassed to say, "that actually interests me too". Here's a way to just do it!

If you find it difficult to voice what you would want on your day, write your "his" and "her" ideas on pieces of paper and then put them in a jar—you can use different colours for each of you, or just use two jars. Then on his nights and her nights you can pick out a piece of paper and do what it says. Again, this psychologically feels easier because you don't have to voice a preference, but you do get your needs met.

5. Have Him Stay Stock Still—and Don't Let Him Talk

Have him lie on his back and tell him that he can't move for ten minutes—and he's absolutely not allowed to talk (he can moan if he wants to, but no words). The benefit? You can explore his body without any feedback from him (well, except that you'll likely see the response you're getting rather obviously). Don't even look at his face if you find it too embarrassing. This lets you actually feel his body or do whatever you want to his body and just get to know it better. If you need to, blindfold him so that he can't see what you're doing, and you feel more free to explore.

Intercourse is actually not the most intimate thing. It's far more intimate to be intentional about touching and teasing and taking time to explore. That shows real interest on your part about learning about him–and that's why it can be embarrassing. If any of us grew up thinking that showing interest in sex was shameful, then to show interest in learning something sexually can be difficult.

6. Play a Game

Here's another way to try new things. Put the things you want to try on a dice, and then roll the dice and do what it says! I've got a Dice Game that you can print out right here.

7. Play Beat the Clock

Here's another fun–and adventurous–one. Using a kitchen timer (or a stopwatch on your phone), make a list of things you'd like to do and then do them each–but only for two minutes. This gives a kind of urgency to what you're doing, but also helps you to relax a little bit because you're changing things up so constantly. There isn't a lot of time to start second guessing yourself or getting nervous!

Here's another variation on the same idea: take him into the bedroom and tell him he can do anything he wants to do–but he only has 5 minutes. So he had better get a move on and have some fun! If he's not finished in that time, then you're going back downstairs (but have pity on him later in the day, or play again in an hour or two).

This is often exciting because you're concentrating on his pleasure, not yours. In that amount of time most women can't reach orgasm, so the emphasis isn't on making you feel good. It's on letting him have as much fun as possible as quickly as possible. So he doesn't have to worry about saving himself or holding something back for you. He can let go! For a lot of women this is a very freeing thing because you see how excited you get him when he only has to care about having fun himself (a lot of men won't even need the whole 5 minutes).

Chapter 15: How to Choose the Best Lube for Sex: Types of Lubricants, Pros and Cons

The truth is, at times sex is not always as romantic as it might seem in your favorite blockbuster movie or on a TV show. Sometimes, it is uncomfortable, uncoordinated, and could use a little sex lube in order to smooth things over. At times, a man is all ready to go but a woman is not just quite there, or she may not be able to stay physically wet during long-lasting sex.

It is worth mentioning that there are many solutions to this common problem, such as using lubricated condoms; however, you will be surprised to know how far you could get with just a standard sex lubricant.

Buying sex lube, especially for women, can be, at best, embarrassing, and on many occasions, downright confusing. Particularly if the only kind of lube you have ever bought is from your nearest drugstore.

And in case you have resigned yourself to using low-quality sex lube (or have avoided it completely), you probably have to experiment with a different type of lube.

What is lubricant used for?

Sometimes, women can experience moderate to severe vaginal dryness. The vagina doesn't lubricate enough, which can lead to discomfort or pain. Vaginal dryness could also occur when women are undergoing chemotherapy, breastfeeding, or when they have been treated for issues like breast cancer.

This is why women prefer more lube than what their bodies provide. A sex lubricant can help in these circumstances. A sex lube is a gel or liquid that women and/or their partners may apply during sexual intercourse to make the vagina, vulva, or anal area wetter.

In addition, lubricant could also be applied easily to a man's penis or various sex toys in order to make them more slippery.

Types of sex lube

When shopping, you have various types of lube to choose from.

The most popular bases for lubes are:

➢ Water
➢ Silicone
➢ Oil
➢ Natural

Hybrid lubes are usually a combo of both silicone and water, and have both elements. Keep in mind that there are several different formulations that can perfectly suit your specific needs.

Water-based sex lubricants

These are considered the most common sex lubricants. They are available in different brands; also, they have no taste, feel like natural lubrication and are less likely to irritate your sensitive skin. In addition, these lubes do not interfere with oral sex. They are also inexpensive and easy to find.

Since these lubes are based on water, they are quickly absorbed by your skin, and this might cause the sex lube to dry out a little quicker.

In order to get rid of this issue, a lot of water-based lubricants have been carefully formulated with high-quality moisturizers like Carrageenan or Aloe Vera. These moisturizers help a great deal. This is because they soothe the skin, reduce dryness, and don't interfere with your sexual experience.

Water-based sex lubes also have the added benefit of being totally condom-compatible, as opposed to a majority of oil-based sex lubes that tend to corrode latex or most old-school petroleum jelly based options.

However, you should watch out for one thing. A lot of water-based sex lubricants contain glycerin, which could lead to infections in women quite easily and can make post-sex clean-up necessary. The great thing is that water-based sex lubes are also compatible with a majority of sex toys; that being said, they are not ideal for the bath or shower (as they tend to wash right off) and they are also not very long-lasting.

Oil-based sex lubricants

In case you are the type who simply cannot be bothered with reapplying the lube at all when you get going, then this sex lube is an ideal gift that will keep you going and going. Oil-based sex lubes feel good and you could easily find them in the kitchen (olive and coconut oil work great).

And here is another pro tip. Oil-based sex lubes can easily double for fun and sexy massage time. However, the downside comes when you are using a latex condom. Keep in mind that this kind of sex lube can increase the risks of a torn or ripped condom, and defeats the condom's purpose in the process as well as your good time.

In addition to that, oil-based sex lubes are also linked to higher rates for infections, like bacterial vaginosis. And another reason you may not want to use these lubes is your expensive sheets. This is simply because oil can stain sheets as well as clothing, making them very difficult to clean up.

Oil-based sex lubes may be considered ideal for couples who are in long-term relationships and do not require condom use and also for people who want to avoid certain preservatives and additives usually present in other lubricants.

Silicon-based sex lubricants

Lubricants based on silicone often contain no water. Note that this may be a big advantage to some while a disadvantage to others.

Silicone-based lubes tend to feel different than most other lubes, mainly since silicone isn't absorbed by your skin, which is not the case with water or oil. This can give a whole new and exciting range of possibilities and spice up your sex life. As silicone is hypoallergenic, a majority of people will not experience a reaction. In addition, this type of sex lubes also tends to last longer.

This may be perfect for you if you are interested in something that has to be reapplied less often and is more long-lasting.

Natural lube

If you are concerned about what ingredients you are putting down there, then do not worry as natural lubes may be right for you. They have really cropped up in the last couple of years. Although it has its downsides, coconut oil is an extremely popular choice when it comes to natural lubes.

That being said, it can increase the risk of condom breakage and stain the sheets, as oils can break down the effectiveness of the latex. You would also want to be a little careful regarding cross-contamination if you are not cleaning the hands while you dip them in a jar of coconut oil that is also used for cooking.

How to use lube for sex

In case you are using a condom, once you put it on, apply the sex lube to the outside of your condom. While a little lubricant on your penis inside the condom maybe good, as well, you certainly do not want there to be too much.

If you are, however, in a relationship and are using other forms of birth control and can skip the condoms, you can apply the sex lube directly to your vagina or penis. Note that lubing these parts is also ideal for foreplay. And in case you are having anal sex, you should focus on thoroughly lubing up your anus. In all cases, you can be liberal with lube, as there is often no such thing as too much lube when you are having anal sex.

What is the best lube for anal sex?

Often, thicker lubes are ideal for anal sex. This is because anal walls are more delicate and thinner compared to vaginal walls, and hence need a sex lube that could keep them slippery and oily in order to reduce the risks of tears and cuts inside your rectum.

Overall, anal sex is deemed especially risky when it comes to STI transmission. This is why condom use is essential (unless you are in a long-term monogamous relationship, and both you and your partner have been tested). Also, this is why it is vital to make sure you use a sex lubricant that is latex-friendly.

Another thing that you should bear in mind is that your anus absorbs water quite quickly and could dry out quite easily when you are using any water-based lube. Hence, silicone-based sex lubes are often the best for anal sex. Basically anything in the kitchen, for example, coconut oil cannot be used with a condom.

Substances you should not use as a lube

You are going to find all types of options in the market when you go lube shopping. These include natural, flavored, warming, and tingling. Although many of these sex lubes could be fun, you should look at the ingredients and also perform a test for the pH value of different over-the-counter products using litmus strips.

Healthy vaginas have a pH level of about 3.5 to 4.5; hence, the sex lube you choose must also be about the same level. This is why you should always pay special attention to all the ingredients listed. And, there are some names you should avoid as they can cause inflammation or irritation.

These include:

> ➢ Nonoxynol-9
> ➢ Glycerin
> ➢ Petroleum
> ➢ Chlorhexidine gluconate
> ➢ Propylene glycol

Bear in mind: it's always better to use a proprietary, tested substance as a lube for sex. This will help you avoid allergies and get maximum pleasure from sex.

Chapter 16: 10 Ways to Use Lube During Sex

Lube is the unsung hero of sex. It's galaxy brain-level sex-having, because it's so obvious, yet so brilliant, and once you know about it, you'll think back on the time before you did as the horrid "before years."

For some reason, lubricant has this fuddy-duddy reputation as something that's only for people who've "dried up." But there's absolutely no truth to that. Lube, in all its glory, is for everyone—as in, everyone should be using it more times than not. And not just using it, but using it creatively.

No shade, but if you're new to the lube world, there are a few things you need to know. First, lubricant can be made from four different materials: water, oil, petroleum, or silicone. Water-based is the safest option if you're using condoms (since it won't break down the rubber), plus, it can be easily washed away from your bodies, sheets, whatever, post-coitus.

Silicone-based lube is great for shower or pool hookups and anal sex because it generally stays slicker for longer and won't wash away in water. Just know some silicone-based lubes can break down condoms, so use a backup birth control method and communicate clearly with your partners about STIs.

Now for the fun stuff: Here are 10 ways you probably aren't but totally should be using lube. Go forth, and enjoy the slippery ride.

1. Use it before sex even happens. Lube has this reputation as being something you pull in off the bench during penetrative sex when a partner is having a harder time maintaining their own lubrication, and this is total BS. Help break this taboo by bringing your new slick friend out during foreplay. Have a partner place some in their palm and grind your vulva and labia against it for a new twist on a hand job for women

2. Use it for a warming massage. The first rule of using warming lube (it heats up with any body-to-body contact or friction) is to never use it without telling your partner first (unless you want them thinking you've just put Icy Hot in their private parts). Other than that, there really are no rules–go forth and heat things up! One suggestion? Use a few dollops on your partner's (or your own) nipples for nipple stimulation that's literally hotter than ever.

3. Use it to amp up his orgasm. During sex with a male partner, dab a few little droplets of lube onto his perineum— AKA the extra-sensitive spot between his scrotum and anus. Just before he orgasms, lightly tap your finger on the lubed-up spot to change the whole damn game and send him over the edge.

4. Use it when you masturbate. Yes, even sex with yourself can be improved with lube. If you have dry hands, no need to use a moisturizing lotion that could contain unwanted chemicals, especially because you don't want those ingredients inside you. Just apply a few drops of a water-based lube to your finger before touching yourself for a smoother feel.

5. Use it when you masturbate with a vibrator. Imagine the electrifying pulse of your favorite vibrator hitting all the right spots. Now imagine using that same toy to gently glide over your clitoris with the same power, but a totally different, more fluid sensation. A dab of lube on a vibrator is a total game-changer. Just be careful: If your sex toy is made of silicone, you'll definitely want to use a water-based lube, since silicone lubes can deteriorate soft rubber.

6. Use it during vaginal intercourse, obvi. There's no wrong way to use lube during intercourse. You can apply it directly to your body, or to the penis or condom itself. My personal rule of thumb is to start with a dime-size dollop and work up from there. Sure, you may encounter a point at which it's too much (he's slipping everywhere, it's dripping excessively on the sheets), but that's easily remedied with a paper towel. You don't want to reduce all the friction, but that threshold is personal for everyone and you'll know it when you feel it.

7. Use it inside the condom. First off, no guy should ever whine about how using a condom "ruins sex." Buck up, my man. But

if your partner is looking for more ways to increase feeling while being protected, Eric Garrison, sexologist and author of Mastering Multiple-Position Sex, has a suggestion. "Many guys complain that a condom diminishes the sensation," Garrison previously told Cosmopolitan.com. "Adding a little lube ups the sensitivity he feels inside the latex." If you put a drop or two inside the rubber before you unroll it, that might unlock a world of feeling, and it should certainly be enough to shut him up.

8. Use it during anal intercourse (obvi). While you might hit a limit of "yeah, too much" during vaginal intercourse, that threshold will be much lower with anal sex, because unlike your vagina, your booty does not create its own lubricant to make things slidey and glidey. SO LOAD IT ON THERE! When it comes to any butt stuff, too much lube and precautions are never enough.

9. Use it during a blowjob. This might sound counterintuitive, but it's true! Sex therapist Gina Ogden, PhD, author of The Return of Desire, previously explained: "Women often use spit, but it can be hard to muster up enough. A flavored lubeprovides enough wetness that your jaw won't get as tired." So there you have it...

10. Use it for a sexy massage. Why not try a body-safe lube during nonsexual foreplay? A few squirts can turn a back

massage from relaxing to "holy hell, your touch is electrifying, can we please have sex right now?"

Chapter 17: How to use a vibrator and sex toys the right way

Unsure how to use a vibrator? Never tried one before? That's totally fine and also, Excited for you to up your masturbation game! Before you start, it's important to know how to use a vibrator in the best possible way. It's not always as simple as picking any old toy, charging it and pressing the 'on' button.

If you've never bought one before, how do you know which type to go for? How do you use them during sex, or even suggest introducing it into sex with a partner? And like, where and how should you use them so they'll feel great?

Know it's completely normal - even for couples

The first thing to realize is that sex toys are now a regular part of many couples' sexual routines. Using a vibe doesn't mean your sex life is rubbish, so banishing your partner's fear of inadequacy should be the first item on your list. Using a vibrator is a fun way of reaffirming your mutual trust, making you more open-minded, intimate and confident with each other's bodies.

FINDING THE RIGHT TOY

Everyone is different and you need to find a vibe that works for your body. There are all sorts that you can choose from, and it can be kind of intimidating if you're not sure where to start.

Bullet vibrators

A great beginner's vibe is a bullet vibrator - these are small, powerful vibrators primarily used for clitoral stimulation. Because of their petite size and easy-to-use shape, bullet vibes are a great choice for a first-time sex toy. They are also highly discreet, quiet and cheap.

The Rocks Off Bamboo bullet vibrator is one of the best, and it's super affordable. It has 10 speed and pattern settings (whereas most standard bullets have only one), and a pointed tip for targeted stimulation - basically it's cheap and feels really good.

Rabbit vibrators

The rabbit vibrator is renowned for introducing women and people with vaginas to what is known as a 'blended orgasm' (i.e. an orgasm that occurs when two erogenous zones are stimulated simultaneously, like the clitoris and the G-spot).

Classic vibes

Classic vibrators are the traditional shaft shape and tapered at the end to hit all your pleasure points. A good one to try for first timers in Annabelle Knight's classic vibrator.

Wand vibrators

Wand vibrators are another favourite. Famed for being the ultimate orgasm tool, these evolved from neck massagers that were designed to relieve tired muscles, until women and vulva-owners discovered how the powerful vibrations were perfect for clitoral stimulation.

If you want something smaller and have a lower budget, Lovehoney's mini wand vibrators are a good beginner's toy.

G-spot vibrators

G-spot vibrators are tilted at the end to help reach the inner front wall of the vagina where the G-spot is located. Je Joue's G-spot bullet vibrator is made from the silkiest silicone and is perfectly crafted to put pressure on - and target vibratrions to - your G-spot.

FIGURING OUT WHAT FEELS GOOD FOR YOU

You can do this by simply choosing your desired vibration pattern and speed, applying some lube to make things nice and slippery, then moving the vibe around the clitoris and labia until you find the place and method of stimulation that feels the best. That's a basic, but extremely enjoyable approach to orgasming with a vibrator.

Get ready to roam

Sure, it seems small on the surface, but you'd be surprised just how much variation there is in the clitoris, especially as it actually extends around the labia beneath the surface. As you become more experienced, you can achieve a fantastic level of precision with a good vibrator.

Some women and people with vaginas say a particular side of their clitoris is more sensitive, while others prefer to stimulate somewhere just above or below it. If you're especially sensitive, you can also try using it outside the labia. By covering the clit, the vibrations are dulled slightly, which gives you a slower build up to orgasm.

Try edging

When you get used to your vibrator, you can try some really exciting techniques such as 'edging.' This is the practice of bringing yourself close to the 'edge' of orgasm but not quite tipping yourself over it. You keep doing this several times until you are in a super-heightened state of arousal and any touch will make you explode. Sounds like fun? Well, it's even more fun with a great vibe.

Really use those settings

Toys have become increasingly sophisticated and come with a whole range of different settings for different users, for timid first timers who enjoy the gentlest vibrations to those who need concrete-smashing power get them off. It's definitely worth trying each pattern and speed setting as you might discover you like a sensation you never thought you would.

Using vibrators during sex

Some of your sexual partners may find this intimidating. So get them relaxed by using the vibe on them first. If your partner's a guy or a male-bodied person, try the nipples, balls, or the sensitive frenulum just under the head of their penis.

Plus, a small vibe like a bullet can be used to stimulate the clitoris during missionary intercourse without getting in the way.

Chapter 18: Captive Bead Ring - Body Piercing Jewelry

A captive bead ring (CBR) is a ball closure ring or captive ball ring. It is like any circle made up of a wire. A bead, which looks like a ball, is fitted into the circular wire. The wire is slightly less in diameter were the bead fits so that it is not movable within the wire and though the circle is open, the bead doesn't fall off. But also the bead can be fit in such a way that it looks like being clamped by the wire.

Science of CBR

The tensile strength of a metal wire is used to hold the bead in place. The wire is made up of surgival stainless steel, niobium or titanium. The bead is made up of colored glass or ceramic or some semi precious stone.

Popularity of CBR

This body jewelry is very popular. When the bead is removed, the jewelry is removed. So the person who wears it has to simply remove the bead. Still the bead will not fall off the ring. Because of the nature of manufacture it does not hold on clothing, hair or furniture, making them a popular choice for piercings, which are still healing. These are closed in shape and have rounded edges.

A Captive Bead Ring or Ball Closure Ring may be is the most popular kind of body piercing jewelry because one can wear it many ways and style it according to one's own choice. It can be worn on the nose apart from being placed at the navel, lips, nipple etc.

Reports suggest that customers go for buying it as nipple jewelry, lip jewelry, nose jewelry, eyebrow jewelry and also for a clit, genital piercing without miding the pain it may cause during sexual interactions.

Different identities

Captive bead ring is called in another name as well. Sometimes it's called BCR (Ball Closure Ring). CBR can be used as a jewelry an as an instrument. It fascinates with its shape. Sometimes it makes terrible appearance to people who are yet to be comfortable with the idea that it may be a piercing jewelry.

Piercing instrument

CBR can be used as a piercing instrument except tongue piercing. Sometimes people like the navel jewelry to be designed in such a way that they prefer to have it pierced by a CBR. CBR piercing makes faster healing.

The gauge size of the bead ring depends on the piercing type and your preferences of a particular design. A small or large ring opener is required to open the bead. For closing the ring, one needs pliers. But these tools are not needed in case of acrylic rings, which have other arrangements, which are, can easily be opened and closed by hands.

Acrylic Captive Bead Rings

One designer who designs Acrylic Captive Bead Rings makes them from 316L Surgical Stainless Steel. Each Captive Ring is precisioned with machine, are hand polished, has round ends and is 100% guaranteed with quality assured.

CBR designs

Any standard shop should have the following jewelry with numerous designs:

> - 18 gauge body jewelry (gauge for nipple piercing)
> - 20 gauge nose rings
> - Captive bell non-piercing
> - 14k gold captive bead ring
> - Double captive ring body jewelry
> - Bead ring
> - Fixed bead ring navel jewelry
> - Nipple ring sizing guide
> - Eeyore belly rings
> - Cartlidge earings

- ➢ Nipple piercing female photo
- ➢ Vaginal piercing jewelry
- ➢ Male genital piercing CBR

The design houses provide different information including infections, crooked naval piercings. They use the highest quality materials like non-alergenic anodized titanium, UV reactive acrylic, 316L Surgical Steel, silver, 14k gold and organic materials.

Caring the piercing

It has to be cared like any other body puncture. The crusts are to be wiped regularly with warm water that is saturated inside a cotton ball. One has to be careful about the wound getting aggravated.

Chapter 19: Myths and Facts About Sex Toys

Health care is an important aspect of our lives. It becomes even more important when we are sexually active. Health care begins with education. We gain knowledge about health care from parents, books, friends, counselors and health care professionals. But we get careless when it is a matter of sexual health. In today's world when the danger of sexually transmitted diseases at a rise we need to take extra care when it comes to sex health. Whether we are fore playing or are into serious sexual activity we need to take care about are decisions and actions.

When we talk about sex and sexual health we should not ignore even what we consider just for fun and pleasure. Yes you have got it right! Sex toys are what we should also take into deep consideration as it is a matter of health.

Sex toys are devices that help you stimulate and give you pleasure during scx. There are numerous types of sex toy available that are made from different materials. The entire sex toys have their own advantages and disadvantages. A lot has been said about some of the material being harmful or dangerous. The reason is that these material have never been clinical studied as sex toys and as such it is not possible to make an exact statement.

There are a number of sex toys available in the markets that have used different materials and need to be taken care differently. There are sex toys made of plastic, silicone and latex.

Silicone dildos what are they. Sex toys made from silicone are also available in different range of shapes and sizes that give you a real feel. They are made of soft material that is chemically inert and hypoallergenic. Silicone sex toys are relatively non porous therefore much easier to clean. These toys warm the body and thus give a realistic feeling.

There are sex toys made of plastic. They are usually hard and yet smooth. But there are a few plastic sex toys that have textured shaft. These toys are ideal for creating vibrations and are more intense in hard plastic than in a jelly vibrator. You can clean them easily. You can use soap, rubbing alcohol, bleach. You can boil them in water, or put them on the top shelf of your dishwasher. If the toy is being used by you on your own and are not sharing and not using it vaginally and anally, you don't need to use condoms with silicone toys.

They can be used alone or with a partner. However, there are many myths in the minds of people relating to them. We try to relate some of the myths and facts below.

Myth1

Sex toys are only for people who have a bad sex life, or no sex life.

Fact 1

Their usage has become common for men and women. Many couples use them during sexual intercourse. It's not only people who have a bad sex life need to use toys for improving their sexual function. Couples who enjoy successful relationships also need to improve their sexual function with regular use of sex toys that can help explore erogenous zones.

Myth 2

They are addictive.

Fact 2

They are not harmful. It may happen that women who use them regularly may get used to them and won't feel adequate arousal with a real penis. It may cause embarrassment to the partner. However, with optimum use, you may not only improve your sexual function, but quality of sex life as well.

Myth 3

If a woman has a sex toy, she won't need a man.

Fact 3

Although many vibrators may resemble a real penis in shape, these can't replace a real penis. With a real penis, you can feel greater joy and pleasure. However, there's no harm in masturbation, as it can improve how you function sexually. Adult toys are also used by many couples during sex to enhance sexual pleasure.

Myth 4

Guys only use them because they can't get any sex.

Fact 4

Sex toys can help you discover your potential for sexual pleasure. Most couples use them during sexual intercourse as it helps to stimulate various erogenous parts. Therefore, they should not be an excuse because you don't have real sex. Masturbation with adult toys can improve your sexual efficiency and sexual stamina.

Myth 5

Sex toys make sex less natural.

Fact 5

Natural sex desired by everyone. It gives both men and women immense sexual pleasure. However, most women are unable to have an orgasm during sex. Some women may fake an orgasm instead. However, sex toys prove extremely handy for occasions when this might happen. With their help, a woman can help stimulate her deepest erogenous zone known as the G-spot. Therefore, it's a complete myth that they make sex less natural.

Myth 6

There are bad and good toys.

Fact 6

Sex toys can improve your sexual function and provide immense sexual pleasure. They can become bad when you don't operate them properly. Before using any toy for sexual pleasure, you should learn to operate it properly. Nowadays, many sophisticated and advanced toys are available on the market. These take extra care of your sensitive sexual parts such as vagina and clitoris.

Myth 7

The more you pay for, the better it is.

Fact 7

It's not always necessary that only the expensive ones give you immense sexual pleasure. Some cheap ones can also give you an equal pleasure. However, the one thing you need to ensure before buying any pleasure object is its design and what material it is made from. Sex toys are inserted deep into erogenous zones like clitoris and vagina of women and anus of men. Therefore, they should be extra fine and soft. You can also get a good quality ones at cheap rates online.

Myth 8

Sex toys are kinky.

Fact 8

Being kinky behind closed doors is not wrong, in fact, is quite normal for couples. Everyone is entitled to enjoy kinky sex and use adult toys when alone. Many couples use them during sexual intercourse for an enhanced sexual pleasure.

Myth 9

Sex toys can cause damage to your body.

Fact 9

It's a complete myth that sex toys can damage your body. It may happen that you may overuse them due to sexual excitement. Therefore, we advise you to have sex in between as well.

Chapter 20: Choosing a Sex Toy - Selecting the Right Material

Sex toys can be made from just about anything, but most are composed of one of the following materials:

Silicone

Silicone toys are non-porous and can be disinfected. Even textured toys are easily cleaned. It warms to the body and retains heat. It is also extremely durable. Because silicone can withstand high temperatures, you can boil silicone toys (as long as there is no vibrator unit inside) for 5-10 minutes or put them in your dishwasher to disinfect them. They also clean well with soap and water. You can use soap, rubbing alcohol, or bleach to clean silicone sex toys (if you are using alcohol or bleach, be careful to rinse thoroughly). Just make sure you clean them thoroughly between uses.

In addition to being durable, silicone toys are nearly hypo allergenic; very rarely do people experience allergic reactions to them. You can use a silicone sex toy with a water based or oil based personal lubricant but do not use silicone based lubricants (e.g. Eros, Wet Platinum, ID Millennium). Silicone is very durable, but can tear easily. Keep sharp edges away from your silicone toys. No hard edges, no snags or imperfections - if you run your fingers over these toys with your eyes closed, you might think you're touching skin.

Remember: It is possible to transmit infections on sex toys that have not been sterilized even if they have been washed. If you are going to share a sex toy with a partner use a condom on the toy to prevent transmission of bodily fluids, or boil your toy before a new person uses it. Non-lubricated condoms are best for silicone toys.

Jelly

Jelly rubber toys are made of soft, porous material that cannot be disinfected. That means these toys aren't safe to share unless you want to use a condom on them, but they're so inexpensive, your partner can just go out and buy his or her own! Jelly toys can be quite nice, at nearly half the price of their silicone sisters. While not as smooth or silky as sex toys made from silicone, jelly toys can still bring you a tremendous amount of pleasure. The secret is water-based lubrication - use lots of it. Jelly rubber sex toys are soft, and usually come in translucent colors. They feel a bit more resilient than the older rubber mixes used to make sex toys. Clean them with soap and water, and store in a cool, dry place away from other objects. If your toy is not waterproof, please take care not to get water in its battery pack or cord. Latex is often an ingredient, which some people are allergic to.

Cyberskin

Cyberskin toys are made of porous material that cannot be disinfected. Use with condoms for safety and to aid in cleanup. Toys made from this material become warm with use and are the closest thing to skin-to-skin sensation you'll find in a sex toy. CyberSkin is also more durable than latex, it can be used in many more and interesting ways, such as cock rings, eggs, and even human-looking robots! The realistic appearance and feel of Cyberskin makes it perfect for a first time toy, or for anyone who wants something more realistic in the bedroom. Great care must be taken if you share a toy made of Cyberskin, the use of a condom is recommended (as with any toy that is shared) to minimize any possible infections being transmitted.

Plastic

Plastic is the big-city cousin of rubber: it's hard, cold and completely inflexible. There are a variety of plastics used to make sex toys. They are non-porous materials and this means they are easier to keep clean, and people are less likely to react to them. These toys are usually suitable for people concerned with allergic reactions or chemical sensitivities. Plastic is easy to clean using a wet cloth and mild soap or preferably a specially designed sex toy cleaner that also helps kill any bacteria. It is advisable however not to submerge any toy that has a motor in any cleaning agent, or use any agent that can cause skin sensitivity or irritation. Plastic vibes aren't a top pick for internal use or in-out thrusting, but they make wonderful clitoral teasers. Try a plastic sex toy if you like the sensation of cool metal and a hard, pulsing vibration.

The Ins and Outs of Sex Toys

When it comes to sex, the once very private conservation is becoming more and more socially acceptable in the public environment. From the best sex positions to how to enhance the bedroom experience, pillow talk is moving out of the bedroom and into the public eye.

While not everyone is comfortable talking about the subject there are many that are absolutely intrigued by these topics. One of the most talked about sex topics is sex toys. These crazy little gadgets, costumes and playful additions to your bedroom experience are becoming so popular that there are stores dedicated to selling these types of products both in public at a storefront and online. There are also many direct sales companies that do home parties allowing fun, intimate girl's night out!

Whether it is male sex toys or female toys, no gender or sexuality is left out of the fun and games if you know what to look for and what is available. Here are some of the most popular toys and gadgets used to enhance sexual pleasure.

Feel the Shake

One of the most popular of sex toys that couples and individuals use is the vibrator. This toy is used to stimulate your sweet spots through mechanical vibrations that range in intensity. Vibrators can be used in a variety of different ways and come in many different styles that work for both men and women.

The most popular for ladies are those vibrators that are used to stimulate the clitoris or the internal walls of the vagina. These two locations are important in that some women orgasm through clitoral stimulation while others need the internal g-spot tickled. Vibrators are a staple of the female sex toys line and chances are you know someone who uses one frequently, even if they don't reveal this little secret.

Tie Me Up

For many men and women, sexuality and a thriving sex life are tied to fantasy and role playing. Among the most popular of these scenarios of escape is bondage or BDSM. In this scenario, one or more partners take on a dominant role while the other is more submissive. The depth and intensity of the playing varies based upon the needs and wants of the partners involved. The toys used in this type of sexual play can be very diverse ranging from strap-ons to vibrators to dildos to butt beads and even sex swings, gags and blindfolds.

Bondage toys include items such as whips, chains, handcuffs, and masks among others depending on the roles you are playing. Fetish Fantasy is one of the top brands in this genre of BDSM collectibles and offers both male sex toys and sex toys for females as well.

Enhancement Additions

There are times in the bedroom when it becomes necessary or wanted to bring in what is missing. Whether it is a new partner or a new outfit, these additions can provide spice to an already existing relationship. The same approach can also be applied to enhancement toys as well. Strap on dildos and those that are utilized manually are two of the most popular that are purchased. While a strap on is a dildo that is affixed to the body for penetration, a dildo tends to be made to be attached to a flat surface or free to be moved about as necessary. These can be great for both gay and lesbian or straight couples and can bring about a new sensation or feeling of excitement into a sexual relationship. Fctish Fantasy and COLT are two brands that stand out as top leaders in this genre of sex toy and may be the missing spice your sex life wants

Chapter 21: Woman's Guide to Safe Sex Basics

Practice safe sex

As a woman, you shouldn't be afraid to take control of your sexual health and safety. Being prepared, being ready, and being safe are healthy and wise. Preventing getting or spreading sexually transmitted infections (STIs), such as HIV, gonorrhea, or syphilis, helps both you and your partners stay disease-free. Plus, smart use of birth control can help you avoid an unplanned pregnancy.

Research your birth control options

Birth control options are expanding. Today, daily pills, monthly injections, vaginal rings, and intrauterine devices are all options for preventing pregnancy if you are sexually active. Talk with your health care provider about your birth control options if you are or may become sexually active. At each yearly check-up, discuss your lifestyle changes and decide if your birth control option is still the right one for you. Also, if your birth control is causing unwanted side effects (such as dizziness or decreased sex drive), work with your doctor to find a birth control option that works better.

Know your status

If you are sexually active or have been in the past, it's important you are checked regularly for STIs. Some diseases that are contracted through sexual encounters do not cause significant symptoms or signs until several weeks, months, or even years after you've contracted them. By the time you find out you have the STI, you may have unknowingly shared it with someone. Likewise, a partner may unknowingly share an STI with you. That's why you should be tested often. It's the only way you'll know for sure if you—and your partner who is tested with you—are clean. Your general practitioner can conduct the test.

Use protection every time

It might seem like trite advice, but the best way to prevent pregnancy and lower your risk for getting an STI is to use barrier protection correctly every time you have a sexual encounter. Male condoms are the most common form of protection. If your partner does not want to use a male condom, you can use a female condom. (More is not better— using both a male and female condom can cause one or both to break). If you or your partner is allergic to traditional latex condoms, polyurethane condoms are available. Also, natural condoms, often made from lambskin, can prevent pregnancy, but they do not protect against HIV or other STIs. You can purchase condoms at most any pharmacy or mass-market retailer.

Communication is key

Be honest about your sexual past, your preferences, and your decision to practice safe sex. This way, you and your partner can communicate openly. It's important that the two of you share your sexual histories so that you can find out about potential STIs or diseases. Some STIs are not curable; you will want to use protection to prevent receiving any incurable STIs from a partner. Also, discussing your past opens up the path to talk about testing for STIs.

Abstain from sex

You can contract STIs from vaginal, anal, and oral sex. The only way to be 100% sure you'll prevent an unplanned pregnancy or an STI is to not have sex, or to abstain. Make a decision to abstain from sex until you're emotionally and physically ready. Share this decision with any partners, too, as a way to keep yourself accountable. Sharing your decision to abstain from sex until you're in a committed, monogamous relationship opens up channels for discussion with your partner and can help the two of you be more honest about your sexual health.

Limit your number of partners

This fact is simple: The more people you are sexually involved with, the more likely you are to get an STI or to get pregnant. Limit your number of sexual partners. Each new partner brings a history of other sexual partners, sexual encounters, and potential infections. If you're not in a monogamous relationship, being smart about your sexual encounters can help keep you safe.

Or better yet, be monogamous

Apart from abstinence, the best way to prevent contracting an STI is to be part of a long-term, one-partner relationship. As long as the two of you remain faithful to one another, you may reach a point in your relationship where you decide to have sex without barrier protection. (If one of you has an STI, you may want to continue using barrier protection, even if you're monogamous, to prevent transmitting the infection.) However, this pact only works if both of you remain monogamous. If your partner begins having sexual encounters outside your relationship, you may contract STIs without knowing it. (2)

Use protection for all types of sexual encounters

You can only get pregnant from vaginal sex, of course, but you can contract an STI from vaginal, anal, and oral sex. For that reason, protection is a must at any sexual encounter. Using male condoms or dental dams can help keep you from contracting an STI, such as HIV, during oral sex. Male condoms can also prevent sharing an STI during anal sex. Both female and male condoms are good for vaginal sex, but do not use them together.

Be careful of the products you use

Don't be quick to use a douche or vaginal wash. These products can remove normal, healthy bacteria—bacteria that could actually help prevent an infection. If you use these washes frequently, you increase your risk of getting an STI.

Use a lubricant when you have sex. Condoms can tear or rip if you or your partner is not properly lubricated. Lubricants can also prevent skin tearing during sex. Open skin is an avenue for sharing STIs. Use water- or silicone-based lubricants, not oil-based lubricants. Oil-based lubricants can actually increase the risk of a condom tearing. Read all directions on the condom box to make sure you're using it properly.

Clean sex toys, too

You and your partner may turn to sex toys as a way to add interest to your relationship. These devices cannot get you pregnant, but they can still spread STIs and other infections. Wash and sterilize any sex toys between uses. You can also use latex condoms on sex toys. This will help keep them clean and reduce the likelihood you'll get an infection.

Safe sex is healthy sex

Sex is not always the easiest topic to bring up with a new partner—or even a partner you've had for a while. It can be uncomfortable, but it's important. Safe sexual practices keep you and your partner healthy. Before your first sexual encounter, it's smart to have a discussion about your behaviors, preferences, history, and choices for protection. Being proactive about this talk helps prevent heat-of-the-moment decisions that can lead to long-term regrets.

What types of birth control are there?

Birth control is the use of various devices, drugs, agents, sexual practices, or surgical procedures to prevent conception or pregnancy.

It enables people to choose when they want to have a baby.

A range of devices and treatments are available for both men and women that can help prevent pregnancy.

Some methods are more reliable than others. How well a method work often depends on how carefully it is used.

The contraceptive pill, for example, used correctly, is over 99 percent effective. However, because people make mistakes, as many as 9 women each year will become pregnant while using it.

This chapter will look at a range of methods of preventing pregnancy. It gives the actual rates of effectiveness, which take into account the possibility of human error.

Fast facts about birth control

➢ Birth control can help people decide when they want to have children.

➢ There are many types to choose from, including different types of barrier, medications, and traditional methods that need no additional resources.

➢ Effectiveness varies and often depends on how carefully the method is applied.

➢ Only a male condom offers any protection against sexually transmitted infections (STIs).

Natural methods

Traditional birth control does not involve any type of device or medication.

Abstinence: Celibacy or sexual abstinence means avoiding sexual intercourse.

Withdrawal: Also known as coitus interruptus, this is when the man removes the penis from the vagina so that ejaculation occurs outside of the vagina. In theory, this prevents the sperm from being deposited in the vagina.

According to the United States Health and Human Services (HHS) Office for Population Affairs, each year, for every 100 women who use this method, 20 may become pregnant.

In other words, withdrawal is about 80 percent effective, but this depends on how carefully and how consistently it is used.

The penis does not need to enter the vagina for pregnancy to occur. It can happen if sperm enters the vagina during foreplay, for example.

Devices

Barrier devices prevent the sperm from meeting the egg. They may be combined with spermicide, which kills the sperm.

Male condom

The male condom forms a barrier and prevents pregnancy by stopping sperm from entering the vagina. It is placed over the penis before sexual intercourse begins. A condom is made of polyurethane or latex.

It can also help to prevent the spread of sexually transmitted infections (STIs).

It is around 82 percent effective. Some 18 women in every 100 may conceive if their partner uses a condom.

Condoms are available from drugstores, supermarkets, and many other outlets. Health providers also supply them, sometimes for free. You can also purchase them online.

Female condom

The female condom, or femidom, is made of polyurethane. It has a flexible ring at each end. One fixes behind the pubic bone to hold the condom in place, while the other ring stays outside the vagina.

Spermicides may be placed in the vagina before intercourse. A spermicide kills sperm chemically. The product may be used alone or in combination with a physical barrier.

The female condom is 79 percent effective. Around 21 women will become pregnant each year with this method.

Sponge

A contraceptive sponge is inserted into the vagina. It has a depression to hold it in place over the cervix. Foam is placed into the vagina using an applicator. The foam is a spermicide that destroys the male sperm, and the sponge acts as a barrier to stop the sperm from reaching the egg.

Between 12 and 24 women out of every 100 who use the sponge may become pregnant.

It is less likely to work if a woman has already had a baby.

The diaphragm

A diaphragm is a rubber, dome-shaped device that is inserted into the vagina and placed over the cervix.

It fits into place behind the woman's pubic bone and has a firm but flexible ring that helps it press against the vaginal walls.

Used with spermicide, it is 88 percent effective. Used alone, it is between 77 and 83 percent effective.

Cervical cap

A cervical cap is a thimble-shaped, latex rubber barrier device that fits over the cervix and blocks sperm from entering the uterus. The cap should be about one-third filled with spermicide before inserting. It stays in place by suction.

It is around 88 percent effective if used with spermicide, and 77 to 83 percent effective without.

Injections

The contraceptive injection, or "the shot," is a progestin-only, long-acting, reversible, birth-control drug. The name of the drug is Depo-Provera, also known as the Depo shot or DMPA.

The shot is injected every 3 months at a doctor's office. It prevents pregnancy by stopping the woman from releasing an egg.

It is 94 percent effective, and the chance of pregnancy increases as the shot wears off. It is important to remember to book another shot after 3 months to ensure its effectiveness.

It does not protect against STIs.

Pharmaceutical types

These range from pills you can take to devices that are inserted by a doctor. You need to see a health provider to obtain most of these types of birth control.

The intrauterine device (IUD)

The intrauterine device (IUD), or coil, is a small, flexible T-shaped device that is placed in the uterus by a physician.

There are two types:

A copper IUD releases copper, and this acts as a spermicide. It can last up to 10 years.

A hormonal IUD contains progestin. It prevents the sperm from reaching and fertilizing the egg by thickening the cervical mucus and thinning the wall of the uterus.

It stays in place as long as pregnancy is not desired.

Depending on the type, it will last for 3, 5 or 10 years. It is over 99 percent effective.

Contraceptive pill

The combined contraceptive pill is taken daily. It contains two hormones, estrogen and progestin. The hormones stop the release of the egg, or ovulation. They also make the lining of the uterus thinner.

It is effective for between 91 and 95 percent of women on average.

Contraceptive patch

This is a transdermal patch that is applied to the skin. It releases synthetic estrogen and progestin hormones.

The patch is worn each week for 3 consecutive weeks, generally on the lower abdomen or buttocks. No patch is worn in the fourth week, to allow for the menstrual period. The patches are readily available.

It is estimated to be 91 percent effective.

Vaginal ring

The contraceptive vaginal ring is a flexible, plastic ring that releases a low dose of progestin and estrogen over 3 weeks. It prevents ovulation and thickens the cervical mucus, so that sperm cannot move easily.

The woman inserts the ring into the vagina for 3 weeks, and then she removes it for one week, during which she will experience a menstrual period.

It is also known as NuvaRing, the trade name for a combined hormonal contraceptive vaginal ring manufactured by Organon.

It is 99 percent effective, but the chance of human error reduces this to 91 percent.

The implant

An implant is a rod with a core of progestin, which it releases slowly. It is inserted under the skin of a woman's upper arm.

The implant is effective for up to 4 years, but it can be removed at any time, and then pregnancy is possible.

It is 99 percent effective in preventing conception, but it will not protect against an STI.

Emergency "morning after" contraception

Emergency contraceptive pills, or the "morning-after pill," may prevent pregnancy after intercourse. It prevents ovulation, fertilization, or implantation of an embryo.

It is different from medical methods of termination, because these act after the egg is already implanted in the womb.

Emergency contraception can be used up to 72 hours after unprotected sex. It is 95 percent effective during the first 24 hours, falling to 60 percent by 72 hours.

Emergency contraception should only be used when primary methods fail.

Some people see it as a kind of abortion, because the egg may have already been fertilized.

Permanent contraception

Sterilization is a permanent method of sterilization.

In females

Tubal ligation: This is a form of female sterilization. The surgeon will cut, block, or burn the fallopian tubes, or a combination of these methods, to seal them and prevent future fertilization.

Tubal implant: A coil is placed in the female's fallopian tubes. Tissue grows around it, blocking the tubes. It can take 3 months to work.

Female sterilization is over 99 percent effective.

In males

Vasectomy: This is surgery to make a man sterile. The tubes through which sperm pass into the ejaculate are cut or blocked. It is over 99 percent effective.

It is sometimes reversible, but with a higher abundance of abnormal sperm, possibly resulting in lower fertility or birth defects.

Myths about birth control

Myths about birth control have proliferated throughout history, but science has put right some common misconceptions.

You cannot get pregnant while you are on your period: It is not true that a woman cannot get pregnant during her menstrual period. She may be less fertile for the first few days of menstruation, but pregnancy is possible, as sperm can live inside the female body for several days.

You cannot get pregnant if you have sex in a hot tub: Sexual intercourse in a hot tub or swimming pool does not prevent pregnancy. There is also no sexual position that prevents pregnancy.

Urinating or douching after sex prevents pregnancy: Douching with any substance after sexual intercourse does not prevent pregnancy.

Non-medical spermicide: Putting toothpaste or seeds in the vagina does not prevent pregnancy and should never be used as a contraceptive.

Sex without penetration, ejaculation, or orgasm is safe: Even if the man does not ejaculate, the woman can become pregnant. Pregnancy is possible any time the penis—or even sperm during foreplay—enters the vagina. A woman can become pregnant whether or not she has an orgasm or is in love with the man.

Breastfeeding protects against pregnancy: A woman can become pregnant while breastfeeding, although the chance is lower.

Using two condoms offers extra protection: Using two condoms or using a tight condom does not offer better protection than one. Using a male and female condom together may increase the risk of pregnancy, as they can shear and tear.

Disease protection

Contraception is a powerful tool both for preventing unwanted pregnancy. Some methods, such as the male condom, can also reduce the risk of an STI. However, it must be used correctly to do so.

No method of birth control is 100 percent effective. Combining two methods, for example, the pill with a condom, offers extra protection as well as some protection against STIs.

It is important to be informed and to use birth control wisely.

Chapter 22: How to Stay Sexually Connected During Infertility Treatment

Most couples know that infertility treatment will take a toll on them physically and emotionally – but many are unprepared for the effect it has on their sexual intimacy. The hyper-focus on fertility can considerably impair desire and arousal in women and can prompt sexual dysfunction in men. The following stressors explain why:

Spontaneity is gone. During infertility treatment, desire is no longer the main reason for love making. Instead, clocks, thermometers, medications, ultrasounds and tests now govern when it is the best time to have sex. Infertile couples have sex to maximize fertility when ovulating, increase sperm counts, and do it in positions that better facilitate sperm to egg. While this amount of planning may be necessary to increase odds of conceiving, it takes a toll: Forty five percent of couples struggling with infertility treatment report that sex "by the clock" is stressful. Sex on demand can cause men to develop erectile dysfunction and premature ejaculation. Women frequently lose desire and have sex without arousal simply to time it correctly.

Medicalization of sex. Couples suffer intimate invasions of their bodies, genitals, and even the details of their sex life. Their sex organs are tested and evaluated for functioning, often with procedures that hurt or even border on humiliation. Hormonal medications that increase ovulation, change the acidity of the vagina, or build the uterine lining often create mood swings that lower desire. At some point in this medical process, the body starts to viewed mechanically, as functional or not, and sexual intercourse is only good if there is a product resulting from it – a pregnancy. The process of helping a couple create a child, ironically, can be dehumanizing.

Changes in sexual definitions of the self. Research shows that women in infertility treatment often view themselves as more feminine if they ovulate in a month but less feminine on months without an egg release. Men can begin to feel less confident about themselves sexually if they are unable to create a child with sexual intercourse, regardless of whether it is due to his sperm count or not. Often when pregnancy results without sexual intercourse but through interventions like intrauterine fertilization or in vitro fertilization and implantation, couples often can view themselves as having failed sexually.

How to recover sexual intimacy during and after infertility treatment:

Acknowledge the crisis. Infertility usually happens within a young marriage or partnership and is often the first and unexpected test of the strength of their joint coping skills. Sexuality and emotional connection are intrinsically inseparable. The couple has to accept their path to pregnancy will be complicated and more mechanical than they might have hoped for, giving each other permission to talk about it and express their disappointment without false reassurances from the other in order to stay connected.

Guard their union against further intrusion. Couples might need to shield one other from hurtful comments or judgment from their families. Likewise, well-meaning people often make incredibly naïve remarks like, "As soon as you stop trying, you'll probably get pregnant." Be selective about who to reveal your plans to as you form your support system. It's hard enough to endure month-after-month with no pregnancy, let alone if you have to report to an audience who is also wondering about the outcome of your sex life.

Separate intimate sex from baby-making. If you can, reserve your bed as the place to try to get pregnant, and make love for fun on the couch, on a rug in front of the fireplace or book a hotel room – anything more creative that relieves you of the "have to sex." Try to have one pleasuring experience a month as a time to talk, touch, reconnect, and reassure each other of your love and desire without the pressure of an outcome.

Share your feelings. Don't try to be strong for your partner. Be open about the worries in your head and ask about your partner's fears. Couples who fall into a cycle of communication with one partner complaining or criticizing and the other defending or withdrawing are at risk for derailing both sex and their relationship. You may want to seek therapy to help become clearer communicators during this stressful season.

The Best Sex Positions - How to Make a Woman Reach Orgasm During Intercourse

Have you ever wondered what the best sex positions for a women to reach orgasm? The so-called love gurus keep this little secret to themselves, but being an amazing lover is all about the positions you have in your repertoire. There are a few sex positions that are guaranteed to thrill her in the bedroom. Try this exciting series of sex positions to give her mind-blowing orgasms that will make you the best lover she has ever had.

Many guys find it difficult to make a woman orgasm from intercourse alone and so they resort to vibrators, rubbing her clit, or oral sex. But this isn't necessary. Wouldn't it be nice to give her an orgasm from sex alone and not have to worry about giving her an orgasm after you've had one and are ready to just sit back in that after sex glow? It is time for you to take the sex positions in your bedroom to a whole new level. It's time for your sex life to become so wild and fun it takes your sex life to a whole new level! You can make her happy by giving her the pleasure she needs to ensure that she is always begging for you. Learn these sexual positions so you can make a woman to reach orgasm during intercourse.

Woman on Top

We call this one the cowgirl because deep down, she loves to be on top. When a women is on top, she feels like she is in control, it's a very emotionally gratifying and sexually stimulating position for her. She is able to rub herself along your cock in exactly the right way to get you against her g-spot insuring her a bed-rocking orgasm. She can also rub her clit against you in the exact way she likes to build up to an amazing combined clitoral and g-spot orgasm. When she gets one of these, she'll climax harder than she ever has before.

Using her PC muscles

When a women does kegel exercises, she strengthens her pelvic muscles and is able to contract and squeeze her vagina around your cock harder. Not only does this make her feel oh so much tighter around you, but it increases the friction and her pleasure too. When a women uses her pelvic muscles, she can often experience a squirting orgasm. Trust me, you haven't lived until you've given a woman on of these.

Missionary

The missionary position (you on top) is a classic for a good reason, it works. This positions lets the two of you gaze into each others' eyes, giving her much greater feeling of intimacy. For women, intimacy equals arousal. The more of an intimate connection she feels between the two of you, the faster and harder she will climax. This doesn't even include the fact that missionary position allows for deep penetration and if you have a penis with an upward curve, you'll also be stimulating her g-spot. This is a sure way to make her groan with pleasure as you take her over the brink.

Hip Rotations

All it takes is for you to stop thrusting and start moving your hips in a circle. As men this isn't the most sexually stimulating way to have sex and is thus perfect for times when you are coming close to climax. Start grinding circles into her, delay your orgasm while building her up for a big one. Women love the hip grind.

Thrust control

This is an old eastern sexual technique. It involves making 8 short, shallow thrusts, followed by one long, deep thrust. This magic technique has you rubbing right against her g-spot with each shallow thrust, while the deep thrust keeps things interesting for both of you. Women love it when a guy can do this. It shows her that he knows what he is doing and that he is making sure she is getting as much pleasure as possible. A generous and skilled lover is key for maximum sexual satisfaction.

The Table

Have her sit on table or counter with her legs apart. The table or countertop should be at the exact height at which you can thrust into her without having to stretch or bend down. This give you a great angle for you to rub her clit. This is also a bit sexier of a position since it's outside of the bedroom, involves you picking her up and taking her somewhere spontaneous. It's impossible to have sex in this position without getting that extra turn on from taking things outside of the bedroom.

The Spoon

Lie on your side with you spooning her and go crazy. From this position you can kiss and bite her neck, pull her hair in for a kiss, or even reach around and caress her breasts and clit. If this isn't ideal for thrusting, simply prop her leg up for a deep penetration that will have her moaning with satisfaction.

Doggy Style

It's raw, it's sexy, and it's dirty. Now it's easy for us men to admit that we love a nice down and dirty raw fuck every once and a while. And even though many women are embarrassed to admit this, it's a lot of girls favorite position for a nice hot fuck. You can be quick and rough in this position, you are guaranteed deep penetration, and she loves to be taken like this. The dominance of a man fucking her while she's bent over begging for his cock will take her to climax and beyond. This is a primal position that can't help but be incredibly sexy. Everyone loves for sex to get a little rough every once and a while, and this is the perfect position to pull her hair and fuck her HARD.

Of course, just like every dick is different, so is every pussy. Not all of these positions may be satisfying to your partner, but if you talk to her about what she likes. You're bound to find at least a few on this list that will give her screaming orgasms.

Conclusion

Good sex is ideal for most people. Here you have a partner who engages in activities that please you and there is mutual satisfaction on both ends. The night ends with two satisfied people who know they have hit a home run.

Great sex is the exception. When people are fortunate to reach this level they find that sex has taken on a whole new dimension. Things occur like multiple orgasms, feelings of total contentment and being totally open and relaxed in that person's presence is the norm. It would be fair to say that most people have not entered into a great sexual relationship with another person.

Some keys to getting to the great sex phase;

1) You need an emotional connection to have great sex - This is both a physical and emotional connection. It requires not only the body but a connection of the heart as well to be great.

2) Forget about casual sex - you can't meet a person in a bar and expect to have great sex. Great sex involves both an emotional and physical connection.

3) Creativity is the key - you must be open and willing to be what your partner needs. No one should be forced to have sex when they don't want to in ways they don't want to do it.

Imagination can make a bedroom a great place to not only play out fantasies, but to enjoy each others company.

Great, mind-blowing sex can be a healing and transformation, making both partners feel lovely, alive, and full of energy, but unfortunately, it's quite rare.

Different complaints about sex that is less than satisfying are selfishness, lack of interest, poor hygiene, low sexual energy, being too quick or slow, being too aggressive or passive, lousy attitude, and overweight.

What makes someone great in bed? The right sexual technique, wanting and knowing how to please each other, a concern for safe-sex, the humor of romantic adventure and playfulness, and being relaxed and confident all contribute to great sex between partners.

All of those things matter, but what can make or break great sex is the energy or spiritual connection between two people. If you pay attention, you'll notice the energy connection is different between every person you meet. The spiritual connection also includes subconscious memories of how your souls knew each other in past lives. Consider the circumstances below metaphoric if you don't believe in reincarnation.

Having great sex doesn't have to be rare; address the source of it, and you'll increase the likelihood of more satisfying sex for both you and your partner.

www.ingramcontent.com/pod-product-compliance
Lightning Source LLC
Chambersburg PA
CBHW060514290526
45791CB00001B/380